UNDERGROUND GOVERNMENT:
THE OFF-BUDGET PUBLIC SECTOR

JAMES T. BENNETT AND THOMAS J. DiLORENZO
FOREWORD BY GORDON TULLOCK
EPILOGUE BY WILLIAM SIMON

This book was made possible by a grant
from the Scaife Family Charitable Trusts.

CATO INSTITUTE

Library of Congress Cataloging in Publication Data

Bennett, James T.
    Underground government.

    (Cato public policy research monograph)
    Includes bibliographical references.
    1. Off-budget government entities—United States.
I. DiLorenzo, Thomas J. II. Title. III. Series.
HJ2052.B46   1983   336.73   83-1940
ISBN 0-932790-37-2

Printed in the United States of America.

CATO INSTITUTE
224 Second Street S.E.
Washington, D.C. 20003

UNDERGROUND GOVERNMENT

CONTENTS

TABLES

FOREWORD

One of the more intriguing aspects of this book is that its impact on the current debate about a constitutional amendment restricting government expenditures or prohibiting deficits is likely to be resented by both sides. Looked at one way, the analysis demonstrates that the amendment will have little success in restraining the growth of government in the long run. Looked at another way, the findings connote that no one should really object to the amendment because government officials will still conduct "business as usual." In essence, Bennett and DiLorenzo say that all that is likely to happen is that government will eventually adopt other forms of spending and deficit finance. But this does not necessarily imply that efforts aimed at constitutional reform are superfluous. Quite the contrary, according to the authors. As they state, what is needed is a better understanding of how, why, and when governments are constrained by constitutions so that more effective constitutional reforms, although never a panacea, may be implemented. In fact, one of the major contributions of this book is to demonstrate how the process of government in a democracy produces an urgent need for such limitations on political behavior.

What we would really like in government is for the decision-makers to carefully evaluate the cost and benefits of any given government activity and undertake it if the marginal benefits are greater than marginal costs and refrain if they are not. Unfortunately, we know no set of institutions which achieves this goal. What we end up with then is a set of second-best restrictions on government behavior which aim at compelling the government to at least not do too badly in these directions. The voting process is one such restriction, constitutional limitations on expenditure are another. Bennett and DiLorenzo demonstrate that the constitutional restrictions have not worked very well in the past, but it should be pointed out that neither have the voting procedures.

Why do we observe politicians spending money under circumstances where the benefit is less than the cost? One would think that their constituents would be hurt by the tax more than they would benefit by the expenditure. Bennett and DiLorenzo follow the current orthodoxy here in pointing out that the benefits, in general, go to small groups while the cost is widely spread. Although a referendum might beat some particular expenditure, it is likely that the beneficiaries from it will remember what happened by the time of the next election, and the widely dispersed victims will not. Politically, it pays.

We are given very nice examples of this. Nelson Rockefeller spent money for projects which the voters had turned down in referenda. The Federal Financing Bank succeeds in making a lot of expenditures in such a way that the voters, in general, will not know they are made, whereas the beneficiaries will be very well aware of it. The attractiveness of this to the politician is, of course, obvious. Further, the politician has a motive to make the process even less clear than it normally would be. Something like the Federal Financing Bank, by reducing the ease with which those voters who will be injured can be deceived, while not reducing the ease with which the beneficiaries can see what they get, increases the probability of gain to the politician from special interest expenditures. Thus, we see a good deal of off-budget work even when there is no constitutional need for it.

The great contribution of this book, however, is to demonstrate that when there are constitutional restrictions, as there are in many states and local governments, they can be evaded by off-budget measures. It should be said that, as a general rule, the use of the off-budget technique somewhat reduces the flexibility with which the politician can handle his funds and that should, to some extent, lower the total budget. Whether this effect offsets the increasing budget effect of muddying the water by the use of this indirect and devious technique is not at all obvious. Thus, there is no theoretical way of saying whether this should increase or reduce the total budget, and implicit in Bennett's and DiLorenzo's work is the view that it doesn't change it very much, which is probably correct.

There is, however, one very difficult problem. It is a problem that runs through almost all of the modern public choice discussion of special interest groups. Why are the special interest groups rewarded by expenditures rather than by tax exemptions? Of course, a great many special interest groups in fact are rewarded by tax exemptions. The most recent "tax reform" bill had as one aspect a whole series of tax exemptions for people who own race horses (obviously, a socially meritorious group). The immense Federal Revenue Code is, to a large extent, simply a collection of special provisions for the benefit of special interests.

Nevertheless, since the budget has grown larger, it is obvious that government has tended to incur deficits not by undercollecting taxes, but by overspending (of course, it does both). Why then, to repeat, do the special interest groups apparently prefer expenditures to exemptions? I would rather have $100 taken off my income tax than receive, say, a payment of $100 for doing some work for the government which is actually only worth $50.

In the United States, the Constitution does make special exemptions for constituent groups rather more difficult than special expenditures. This is not necessarily true with state and local governments, however, and it is certainly not true in such a place as England, which does not really have a constitution. Since the general pattern of expenditures is the same in the United States as in England, Japan, Israel, etc., presumably there is something in the political structure which leads to expenditures somehow or other being a better payoff to interest groups than tax deductions. I suggest that this is an important research problem for the future.

Nevertheless, the Bennett and DiLorenzo book makes a major contribution to our present knowledge. Looked at from the standpoint of the scholar, the demonstration of the size of these off-budget expenditures is significant. But the data and insights that will be useful in further research are perhaps the most important contributions of the book. From the standpoint of the public-spirited citizen, the book is likely to arouse indignation. The indignation is probably good for the citizen, and certainly if a great many citizens are made indignant, it will be good for the polity.

GORDON TULLOCK
Center for Study of Public Choice

PREFACE

Our interest in the "underground government" is by no means accidental. Some months ago, near the main entrance to George Mason University, a construction project was underway on a most curious building. The structure, it appeared, was to be constructed underground with strange, stack-like projections from the roof to bring sunlight into the interior. When the building was completed, grass was planted on the roof along with a sprinkling of shrubs to break the monotony. The edifice is well-hidden and resembles a bunker. We were curious about who would build and occupy such a novel (and obviously expensive) structure. Investigation revealed the tenant to be the Fairfax County Housing Authority. This finding raised more questions than answers. Fairfax County has widespread "authority" over housing construction, housing inspections, zoning, and other matters, but inquiries indicated that the Authority itself had no concern with such affairs. Scholarly inquisitiveness prevailed and this book is the result. Although no explicit mention is made of the Fairfax County Housing Authority (or, for that matter, of the county's water, industrial development, or other authorities), it is not because of any lack of interest in these specific organizations, but because they are rather small fish in a very large pond. The facts that came to light about the organizations in Fairfax County convinced us that they were not so different from many others across the nation.

As our research progressed, we were amazed at how little had been done on the subject of off-budget activities of government. Even though some attention has been given to off-budget borrowing of the federal government (stimulated by the "crowding out" controversy and massive federal deficits), the local and state governments throughout the United States have made a science of this type of financing for more than three quarters of a century. We believe that the taxpayer should be seriously concerned about the operating methods of all levels of government and especially about off-budget devices for evading restrictions on taxation, expenditure, and debt. The story that unfolds in this book should disturb those who believe that a balanced budget amendment is the panacea for a federal government that is increasingly out of control.

A conscious effort has been made to present the material in a light and occasionally lively manner. We have found that heavy-handed moralizing amply laced with esoteric economic jargon produces few results other than boredom; moreover, some of the antics of the off-budget enterprises that are reported in case studies have such a "Malice in Blunderland" quality that it seemed fruitless to attempt to give them an air of dignity. We hope to have imparted to the reader a sense of the pleasure that we have derived from this undertaking as well as an appreciation of the fact that much more work remains to be done on this subject.

We wish to acknowledge the contributions and assistance of others to this research effort. Mrs. Risa Crews and Mrs. Helen Winter typed the manuscript; Mr. John Dolan, Ms. Karla Springer-Hamilton, and Ms. Analia Castagnino, Scaife Research Fellows in the Economics Department at George Mason University, collected much of the data. Research support provided by the Earhart Foundation, the Media General Foundation, the Sarah Scaife Foundation, and the National Federation of Independent Business is gratefully acknowledged. Our interest in and understanding of "underground government" has been enhanced by our association with many other individuals who are concerned about the growth and expansion of the public sector, including Gordon Tullock, James Buchanan, Yale Brozen, D. Tennant Bryan, Alan S. Donnahoe, William Niskanen, and participants in a Cato Institute "Policy Forum" on off-budget government spending. We are indebted to each and every one of these individuals, but absolve them from any shortcomings in this work—any mistakes are entirely ours.

James T. Bennett
Thomas J. DiLorenzo

I. Going Underground

The Underground Private Sector

Considerable attention has recently been given to the "underground economy," the phrase used to describe private sector activities that are not recorded in the official economic statistics reported by federal, state, and local governments. When used in this context, the term "underground" carries a stigma with illegal and immoral connotations. The economic transactions conducted in the underground economy are, indeed, sometimes illegal, for these include, among others, payments for prostitution, drug dealing, bribery, loan sharking, and smuggling. The reporting of such activity could lead to prosecution and possible imprisonment of the participants so that there has long been an aversion to reporting income or employment arising from such sources. Much of the income generated in the economic underground is not illegal—rather, income and employment on legitimate economic transactions are not reported solely for the purpose of tax evasion. Payments in cash and barter (trade) are exceedingly difficult to trace and, to avoid paying taxes, workers may fail to file income tax returns or may understate their income on the tax returns that are filed. The American humorist and political pundit, Will Rogers, accurately observed that "The income tax has made more liars out of the American people than golf has."

The underground private sector can hardly be regarded as a new phenomenon; after all, prostitution is commonly acknowledged as the world's "oldest profession." The marked interest in the underground economy has been spurred by the recognition that this type of economic activity has not only become widespread but has also been growing very rapidly. As might be expected, it is extremely difficult to measure accurately the dimensions of unreported economic activity, but a number of attempts using a variety of techniques and assumptions have been made. In an early study, Peter Gutmann estimated that the size of the underground economy was about $176 billion in 1976 and approximately $220 billion in 1978.[1] Edgar Feige of the University of Wisconsin

---

[1]Peter M. Gutmann, "Statistical Illusions, Mistaken Policies," *Challenge* (November/December, 1979), pp. 14–17.

1

performed a somewhat different set of calculations to show that the size of the underground economy was as large as $369 billion in 1976 and over $700 billion in 1978.[2] According to Feige's work, the underground economy was about 20 percent of the measured value of all goods and services produced in 1976 and over 26 percent of the total economy in 1978.[3] A more detailed and disaggregated study by Simon and Witte put the size at about $174 billion in 1974 with a growth rate of about 10 percent per year.[4] Even the Internal Revenue Service has recognized the existence of the economic underground and has placed the federal tax loss for 1981 at about $95 billion—a sum that would significantly reduce the federal deficit if the tax revenue could be ferreted out from reluctant taxpayers.[5]

The underground private sector is important for a number of reasons. First, because economic data do not include these off-the-books transactions, the reported levels of income, saving, employment, and productivity are all underestimated. Although there is no general agreement on the exact size or the rate of growth of underground transactions, there is ample agreement that this segment of economic activity is large enough to distort seriously measures of economic activity. If underground employment and income were to be counted, economic growth rates for the U.S. economy would be higher and the economy would appear to be much more robust and healthy than published data indicate. Second, public policy based on biased economic statistics is likely to be overstimulative in an attempt to cure unemployment that does not in fact exist and to raise incomes that are higher than actually reported. Third, and most important from the perspective of this study, the underground economy is a direct response to the burden of taxation and may be viewed as the ultimate stage of the "tax revolt." No action on the part of the taxpayer in response to ever-increasing tax demands is as dramatic and decisive as a flat refusal to pay the amounts demanded by the insatiable public sector.

Americans have long been suspicious of government and have taken, at best, a jaundiced view of politicians. Since the nation's independence, gained under the rallying cry of "no taxation without represen-

[2]Edgar L. Feige, "How Big Is the Irregular Economy?" *Challenge* (November/December, 1979), pp. 5–13.

[3]Ibid.

[4]Carl P. Simon and Ann D. Witte, *Beating the System: The Underground Economy* (Boston: Auburn House Publishing Co., 1982), esp. pp. 285–294.

[5]See "The Underground Economy's Hidden Force," *Business Week* (April 5, 1982), pp. 64–70.

tation," tax revolts have flared at the local, state, and federal levels throughout our history. None of the episodes has exhibited the flamboyance of the nation's best-known tax rebellion, the Boston Tea Party; the skirmishes between politicians who wish to expand the public sector and taxpayers who must bear the cost have largely been confined to the ballot box. The rapid growth of the underground private economy in recent years is significant precisely because it is an indication that taxpayers have become disillusioned with the results that have been achieved in reducing the burden of government through the voting process. Apparently, the notion of "throwing the rascals out" in an election produces very little change—one set of rascals is replaced with yet another. As documented in Chapter II, the tax burden on the American people has grown relentlessly during the past 50 years at all levels of government regardless of the party or politicians in power. The tax burden is only part of the problem; discontent also arises from the complexity of the tax code, which has become so incomprehensible that neither the taxpayer nor the tax collector can understand its mysteries. Millions of Americans must obtain "professional" help in filing their tax returns—a ritual which adds insult to injury. It is not surprising that public opinion polls have repeatedly shown widespread public dissatisfaction with government in general and politicians in particular. The public, it appears, ranks the veracity of public officials on a par with used car salesmen.

A recent manifestation of the tax rebellion is California's Proposition 13, passed in June of 1978, to provide relief for property owners; an East Coast version, Massachusetts' Proposition 2½, followed. Though widely heralded in the news media as a "new" phenomenon in the tug-of-war between government and the taxpayer, such tax-limitation initiatives are hardly new or innovative. For decades, there have been constitutional or statutory constraints on taxation, expenditures, and debt in many states and in most localities. The more recent episodes of taxpayer uprisings are merely testimony to the fact that past efforts to control government expansion have been, at best, successful only in a very limited way and, at worst, largely ineffective in restraining the public sector's appetite for the taxpayer's income. Although constitutional restrictions on federal debt have never been imposed in the U.S., the prospect of very large (and rapidly growing) federal deficits has stimulated great interest in such a measure to control the excesses of the national government. More than 30 states have called for a constitutional convention to adopt a balanced budget amendment. For more than half a century, presidential candidates have consistently campaigned on a balanced budget platform and yet, with rare exception, federal expenditures have always exceeded federal tax receipts.

All individuals, including public officials, are alike in that they act in their self-interest; a rational person will attempt to increase his income, prestige, and sense of self-worth regardless of whether employed in the private or the public sector. In short, individuals respond to incentives by seeking the "carrots" of reward and by trying to avoid the "stick" of punishment. The incentives in the public sector, however, are vastly different from those in the private sector. Success for the public official can be achieved through the growth of government. As the public sector expands, jobs are created which can be given to political supporters and an increase in the scope and size of government enhances the prestige and power of the politician. The ability of the politician to use the machinery of government to bestow favors on special-interest groups that will, in turn, provide votes and campaign contributions for the next election battle has played an important role in the expansion of the public sector. Favors are not free and eventually the taxpayer must foot the bill in one form or another. An innate conflict develops between taxpayers and politicians about the division of the "economic pie."

All individuals object to some degree to constraints on their behavior. Tax increases reduce disposable income and limit the spending options of taxpayers. As taxes rise, more and more individuals become disenchanted and rebel in one way or another against the confiscation of income by government. When tax evasion becomes widespread, the social stigma against cheating on one's taxes is reduced ("everyone does it"), creating another kind of tax "rebellion." The successful politician is well aware of public sentiment toward government and especially the voters' view of taxes. Few have attained elected office on a platform calling for tax increases or greater public debt. However, the politician dislikes constraints imposed on the actions which enhance his self-interest as much as anyone else so that any taxpayer revolt poses a major challenge to those in the public sector.

The Underground Public Sector

Both the tax revolt and the underground economy have been subjected to extensive examination by scholars and the popular press, but the focus of such studies has been the taxpayer and the private sector; very little attention has been given to the public sector response to expenditure/tax/debt limitation initiatives. There is no doubt that constraints on government behavior pose a major threat to politicians, public-sector employees, and powerful interest groups which benefit from political largesse. Budget cuts endanger the income, power, perquisites, and prestige of politicians and bureaucrats. It is unrealistic to expect even grudging acceptance of fiscal restraints from those in the public sector even though the voter has clearly expressed a preference for less taxes and less government spending and borrowing. Typically, the immediate response of a public agency to proposed budget cuts is some variant of what can be referred to as the "Washington Monument syndrome." When faced with a budget reduction, the National Park Service immediately announced that such cuts could only be accommodated by closing the Washington Monument, the most popular tourist attraction in the nation's capital. This tactic has become the stock-in-trade of every federal, state, and local politician and bureaucrat. Police and fire services are always targeted for reductions with any municipal budget difficulties; hospitals and educational services are generally earmarked for curtailment by the states. Rarely, if ever, is there any admission that real economies can be achieved by reducing administrative overhead, by contracting out services to the more efficient private sector, or by eliminating waste and fraud. These threats of serious disruptions in essential services are, of course, intended to bring the taxpayer "to his senses" so that measures to limit government will fail to win voter approval. Such strategies were employed widely in both California and Massachusetts to forestall the passage of tax limitation measures. In each case, however, voters rejected these claims by public officials and demanded fiscal reform.

The "Washington Monument syndrome" can be regarded as the last-ditch effort of public officials to deflect a rising tide of voter resentment against the perceived excesses of the public sector. As all astute politicians are well aware, it is far better to avoid such confrontations than to risk the wrath of the voter. Just as the private sector has "gone underground" in an effort to protect income from expropriation, the public sector has done the same to conceal the expansion of the public sector from the taxpayer. And this "underground government" is the subject of our study.

The mechanics of going underground are deceptively simple for the public sector. As explained in Chapter III, a state or local governmental body merely obtains a corporate charter for an independent entity which can operate "off budget." The spending, borrowing, employment, and other activities of Off-Budget Enterprises (OBEs) do not appear in the budgets or the official statistics of the municipality, county, state, or group of political jurisdictions that created the OBE. The debt of such quasi-public firms does not require voter approval and, more importantly, is not subject to statutory or constitutional debt restrictions. In effect, the OBE device permits the politician to be a magician: Public sector activities can be made to disappear by the simple expedient of a corporate guise which moves the operations off the books and beyond the control and scrutiny of the taxpayer. Without doubt, Houdini would have been envious. Moreover, the OBE has features which the politician can exploit far more effectively to further his advantage than if the activity were conducted on-budget. The creation of an OBE immediately brings into existence a number of interest groups that may be manipulated for political gain and profit. Although the off-budget device has been in use throughout the United States on a broad scale for about half a century, the general public knows little about the causes and the consequences of such contrivances; even today statistics on OBEs are either not collected or carefully concealed.

The consequences of OBEs are best illustrated by the machinations of America's inveterate politician, Nelson Rockefeller, during his terms as governor of New York. Frustrated by voters who repeatedly rejected the bond referenda required by the state constitution, Rockefeller raised the use of off-budget spending to an art. As explored in detail in Chapter IV, Rockefeller's grandiose designs were not to be diverted or delayed by such casual considerations as voter preference. Numerous OBEs were created by the state legislature, at the governor's insistence, to undertake a bewildering variety of activities (including horse-breeding farms) and to issue a massive amount of debt. In theory, taxpayers are not liable for the repayment of principal and interest on bonds floated by OBEs. Rockefeller's excesses in the credit markets were so extreme, however, that it was necessary to create the concept of "moral obligation" debt to avoid a stampede of lenders away from bonds issued by the OBEs of New York State. Though not *legally* required to pay the interest and principal of off-budget bonds in the event of default, the taxpayers were deemed to be *morally* obligated to do so by the courts after attorney John Mitchell (of Watergate fame) devised suitable wording for the indentures under which the bonds were issued. The case studies clearly demonstrate that Rockefeller did nothing by halves, and when bankruptcy did occur, he had departed the state for a higher political office in the nation's capital. His legacy and the debt of the OBEs chartered during his terms of office live on and will haunt the taxpayers of New York for decades to come.

The role of OBEs in the economy of New York State is perhaps unique: No other state has adopted the off-budget finance of so many projects on such a vast scale. Yet Rockefeller's regime demonstrated what could be done off the books if determined effort was made to exploit the technique to its full potential. The recent history of New York may be a portent of similar actions in other states if the tax revolt intensifies; if this happens, the omens for the taxpayer are indeed ominous.

Chapter V will show the prevalence of OBEs at the local level. In Pennsylvania alone, there are about 2,500 of these quasi-public enterprises that are engaged in activities ranging from the operation of airports to the construction and maintenance of zoos. As is true of OBEs at the state level, there are no accurate statistics on the total number of off-budget enterprises at the local level of government—statistics are not generally collected or reported. Two facts can be surmised from the volume of OBE debt outstanding and new-debt issues of these entities at the local level: (1) Municipal OBEs issue vast amounts of debt and, (2) the amount of new security sales by off-budget enterprises has been rapidly increasing. The federal government has actively encouraged both states and municipalities to engage in off-budget operations by providing grants-in-aid directly to this type of entity, bypassing regular units of government that operate on-budget. The evidence clearly demonstrates that when tax or expenditure limitations are imposed on local governments, the pace of off-budget activity accelerates: The tax revolt is more likely evaded than accommodated by politicians. Two brief case studies will illustrate the wheeling and dealing that can be accomplished under the rubric of an OBE. The financial problems of New York City are well-known, but the role played by OBEs in creating the fiscal mess is by no means fully understood or appreciated. The second case study deals with the still-brewing difficulties of a West Coast OBE located in Washington State, the Washington Public Power Supply System, aptly known as "Whoops." Formed by a consortium of public power districts in the state, Whoops set out to construct five nuclear power plants. To date, no electricity has been generated, construction at some of the plants has been suspended, billions of dollars in debt has been issued, and the utility bills of electric power consumers have skyrocketed. Whether established at the state or local levels, the potential for financial disaster is very real in the world of OBEs, and the taxpayer, in one form or another, must bear the cost.

A particular type of OBE is known as an Industrial Development Authority (IDA) which is formed by local governments or states to encourage economic development of a city, county, region, or state. In theory, IDAs issue tax-exempt bonds at below-market rates of interest, which are backed by the credit of the company that receives the proceeds of the loan to build a plant or facility. Although touted on the basis of aiding small business, many of the recipients have been giant corporations. This type of financing has been so extensively used by the McDonald's fast-food chain that the debt instruments are referred to in financial circles as "burger bonds." Chapter VI discusses the rhetoric and reality of the industrial revenue bond, the most rapidly growing type of off-budget debt instrument.

Off-budget spending is a relatively new phenomenon for the federal government. This observation is hardly surprising in view of the fact that neither statutory nor constitutional limits have been placed on the spending or borrowing proclivities of federal politicians. The Budget Act of 1974, however, did attempt to introduce a more systematic approach to the federal budgeting process, and the inception of off-budget operations occurred at the same time. Since then, as the evidence in Chapter VII indicates, the off-budget financing of the federal sector has grown at an astonishing rate. Though little known (and unlisted in the federal government telephone directory), the Federal Financing Bank is the vehicle through which tens of billions of dollars of off-budget debt is processed each year. As demands for constitutional constraints on deficit spending increase, it is to be expected that off-budget finance will become more attractive at the federal level. Despite its professed distaste for fiscal subterfuge, the Reagan administration placed the Strategic Petroleum Reserve off-budget.

There is cold comfort in the knowledge that OBEs and their off-budget operations are not limited to the United States. These entities, in various guises, are found throughout the industrialized world and even in less-developed countries. In Britain, such organizations are referred to as "Quangos," an acronym for quasi-autonomous nongovernmental enterprises. In fact, the origins of the whole notion of revenue bonds, the lifeblood of off-budget enterprise, can be traced to toll bridges in Renaissance England. Tolls were pledged to pay interest and principal on bonds issued to construct bridges. If anything, the boundaries of the public sector in European nations are much more indistinct than in the United States, since in such countries as Britain, France, and Italy, whole industries have been nationalized. In any event, the material presented in Chapter VIII supports the conclusion that politicians all over the world are addicted to expanding the public sector, and the off-budget device has been useful in helping them to achieve their goals.

The final chapter explores in detail the policy implications of this research. Stated simply at the outset, two major conclusions emerge: First, published data on the size and growth of the public sector greatly understate the true amount of employment, spending, and borrowing undertaken by government at all levels; second, statutory and constitutional restrictions on the behavior of politicians may be an important step in bringing government under control, but it is by no means a surefire solution to the problems of the taxpayer. Although it might seem trite, it is nonetheless true that the taxpayer must be eternally vigilant about the activities of the public sector if economic freedom is to be preserved.

Our objective is not only to explain what off-budget enterprises are and how they operate, but also to raise questions about why such entities exist in great numbers and their economic consequences. For example, if the activities of OBEs are appropriate for the public sector, why shouldn't they be treated as just another part of the government, i.e, on-budget? The answers to such questions provide useful insights into the *modus operandi* of the body politic. Throughout the book, case studies are used to expand upon the themes developed; admittedly the foibles of the OBEs exposed, especially in terms of their financial functions, may not necessarily be representative of "typical" OBEs throughout the nation, but they are indicative of the potential excesses that can occur. We make no claim that the work here is by any means an exhaustive analysis of off-budget government, for such an effort would require an enormous amount of basic data collection and interpretation—a difficult, if not impossible, and very costly undertaking. Our goals will have been achieved if others are stimulated to engage in research in this area.

II. Politicians, Public Expenditure, and Public Debt: The Ingredients of Tax Revolts

The Political Economy of Public Expenditure

Benjamin Franklin's well-worn dictum that nothing in life is certain beyond "death and taxes" has withstood well the test of time for more than two centuries. Franklin might have accurately added that tax increases were also a virtual certainty, for in the past five decades, taxes imposed by federal, state, and local governments have taken a growing share of the average worker's income. One would be hard-pressed to suggest that such trends were purely accidental. Since politicians play a major role in raising and spending public sector revenue, in order to understand the growth in the burden of taxation, it is necessary to explore the motivations of politicians and the relationships between politicians and voters.

For the politician, income, prestige, power, and perquisites are derived from only one source: tenure in public office. This observation has two important implications: First, the major goal of every politician is to remain in office; and second, since the planning and performance of the politician is geared primarily to success in the next election contest, there is an innate bias toward a short-term time horizon. To remain in office, the politician must appear to satisfy the needs of his constituents by providing benefits which are concentrated among his supporters while the costs are widely dispersed among all taxpayers and, preferably, deferred in time. Politicians are well aware of voter/taxpayer attitudes toward government which may be best described as a love-hate relationship: The public loves the services provided, but hates to pay for them via taxes. National surveys of citizens have repeatedly shown that Americans are strongly in favor of reductions in taxes, but at the same time support existing welfare-transfer programs and even the extension of these programs, particularly in the area of health care.[1] If attitude surveys are taken seriously, taxpayers are strong believers

[1]For a discussion and summary of such surveys, see Seymour Martin Lipset and William Schneider, "Lower Taxes and More Welfare: A Reply to Arthur Seldon," *Journal of Contemporary Studies* IV (Spring 1981): 89–94.

in the "free lunch,"and politicians who appear to be able to provide something for nothing are likely to be highly successful at the polls.

Campaign promises proliferate in every contest, and inevitably many are broken—a fact which has contributed significantly to the distrust and suspicion directed toward government programs and public institutions. One promise that is rarely made (by a victorious candidate) is that taxes will be raised substantially in order to pay for benefits provided.[2] Once in office, however, the public official must deliver in some way on pledges made during the campaign or risk being discredited by an opponent in the next election. At this point, the ideal politician becomes a magician who is able to produce something from nothing. Increases in the quantity or quality of public services without corresponding increases in taxes can be achieved by borrowing.[3] Debt is a politician's delight, for it permits large amounts of spending to occur immediately (i.e., during the politician's current term of office) with the problems associated with repayment spread over a long period in the future (perhaps even when someone else is in office). Deferred payments are always attractive to elected officials; witness the fact that pension plans in the public sector are typically far more generous than in the private sector. The budgetary impact of increased pension benefits for current employees is not evident until many years in the future, but an outright wage increase for public employees produces an immediate effect on government outlays.[4] There is, then, a strong political rationale for substituting improved pension benefits for higher wages and salaries.

Our early politicians apparently learned well the lessons of the first tax revolt that culminated in the Revolutionary War. Until the 1820s, government was limited in scope and unintrusive, debt was modest

[2]One can only conclude that "supply-side economics" is the most appealing notion ever invented for politicians. The central thesis is that enormous economic benefits can result from substantial *cuts* in taxes, which will encourage savings and work.

[3]It is also possible, but highly unlikely, that the government entity could have a budget surplus so that the same level of taxation could provide more or better services. Budget surpluses are rare—every politician has an incentive to spend as much as possible to court votes—and dangerous as well: The Proposition 13 movement in California was undoubtedly fueled by the existence of a large surplus (about $5 billion) at the state level, which some individuals had proposed using for rather dubious purposes, like a state space program.

[4]The chickens do, eventually, come home to roost. The pension plans of New York City had become so overly generous that the city was (and, many would argue, still is) on the verge of financial collapse. See, for example, Wyndham Robertson, "Going Broke the New York Way," *Fortune*, August 1975, pp. 144–149, 212–214.

and grew very gradually, and taxes were exceptionally low. For example, in 1825, Massachusetts was almost debt-free, its annual expenditures were less than $200,000, and the per capita state tax was only 35 cents—the lowest in the state's history. Ohio spent only $77,000 in 1822.[5] Tax collection systems were rudimentary; considerable income for the public sector was derived from the sale of public lands; and, as strange as it may seem today, individuals often made gifts to the government to pay for some services such as schools. Prior to 1820, the states had incurred almost no liabilities, a truly remarkable condition that did not long exist.

In the 1820s, a great drive was undertaken to provide internal improvements to expand the economic infrastructure of the states by providing financial institutions and transportation links. A canal-building boom developed, largely spurred by the great success of the Erie Canal linking Lake Erie to the Hudson River. State governments took an active role in providing financing for these projects, and most of the state constitutions adopted in the 1820s contained directions or permission for the legislature to encourage internal improvements. States actively borrowed to finance canals, banks, railroads, roads, and other ventures, as shown in Table 1. Debts began to grow very rapidly: ". . . in 1820 these were almost $13,000,000; in 1830, over $26,000,000; and in 1835, over $66,000,000. During the next five years they trebled, reaching $170,000,000 in 1838, and $200,000,000 in 1840."[6] Much of this debt was sold to foreign investors.

In theory, the borrowings were to be repaid from income derived on the investments rather than from tax levies. The building boom, however, led to gross overinvestment in projects, and outright fraud was common. Many of the investments were unprofitable and had to be abandoned. Illinois, for example, had spent $4,000,000 to build a dilapidated stretch of railroad which eventually sold at auction for $21,100.[7] The borrowing bubble burst in the panic of 1837. Many states could not repay their creditors and several simply repudiated their debt. A committee of the Mississippi legislature declared the whole mess to be unconstitutional and refused to pay; other states instituted heavy tax-

[5]George Rogers Taylor, *The Transportation Revolution: 1815–1860* (White Plains, N.Y.: M.E. Sharpe, Inc., 1951), p. 373.

[6]Ernest Ludlow Bogart, *Economic History of the American People* (New York: Longmans, Green and Co., 1936), p. 326.

[7]Albert Fishlow, *American Railroads and the Transformation of the Ante-Bellum Economy* (Cambridge: Harvard University Press, 1965), p. 190.

Table 1
STATE DEBTS UP TO 1838
(millions of dollars)

States*	Banks	Canals	Railroads	Roads	Misc.	Total
Alabama	7,800	—	3,000	—	—	10,800
Arkansas	3,000	—	—	—	—	3,000
Illinois	3,100	900	7,400	—	300	11,700
Indiana	1,390	6,750	2,600	1,150	—	11,890
Kentucky	2,000	2,619	350	2,400	—	7,369
Louisiana	22,950	50	50	—	235	23,285
Maine	—	—	—	—	555	555
Maryland	—	5,700	5,500	—	293	11,493
Massachusetts	—	—	4,290	—	—	4,290
Michigan	—	2,500	2,620	—	220	5,340
Mississippi	7,000	—		—	—	7,000
Missouri	2,500	—	—	—	—	2,500
New York	—	13,317	3,788	—	1,158	18,262
Ohio	—	6,101	—	—	—	6,101
Pennsylvania	—	6,580	4,964	2,596	3,167	27,307
South Carolina	—	1,550	2,000	—	2,204	5,754
Tennessee	3,000	300	3,730	118	—	7,148
Virginia	—	3,835	2,128	355	343	6,663
Total** —	52,740	60,202	42,871	6,619	8,475	170,357

*The seven other states that belonged to the Union had no debt; namely, Connecticut, Delaware, New Hampshire, New Jersey, North Carolina, Rhode Island, and Vermont.

**Totals may not be precise because of rounding.

SOURCE: E. Bogart, *Economic History of the American People* (New York: Longmans, Green, & Co., 1936), p. 326.

ation in order to pay off their debts, if only in part.[8] The states appealed to the federal government to assume responsibility for all state borrowing outstanding, but the effort failed. To say the least, investors both at home and abroad were concerned about the profligate borrowing by

[8]Edward C. Kirkland, *A History of American Economic Life,* 3rd. ed. (New York: Appleton-Century-Crofts, Inc., 1951), p. 277. Additional information relating to this fiscal fiasco may be found in B. U. Ratchford, *American State Debts* (Durham, N.C.: Duke University Press, 1941), chaps. IV and V.

state governments—not to mention the taxpayers whose taxes were raised dramatically. To avoid future excesses, soothe taxpayer frustrations, and restore investor confidence in their bonds, constitutional limits on debt were imposed at the state level. As new states were formed, debt limits were also incorporated into their constitutions so that the bond offerings of these new entities would not be at a competitive disadvantage in the capital markets. Such impediments to borrowing still exist. For example, more than one-third of the states mandate that special elections be held for voters to approve general obligation borrowing; i.e., the issuance of notes or bonds backed by the "full faith and credit" of the state which guarantees repayment of the debt through its taxing power. Almost one-half of the states have constitutional provisions that place specific dollar limits on the amount of general obligation debt that the state can issue. In some cases, the specific debt limit is tied to property values. When the debt ceiling is reached, every new bond issue requires an amendment to the constitution. Less than 20 percent of the states permit the legislature to incur debt without special elections, but even then, several states require special majorities such as three-fifths or two-thirds of the legislature to approve borrowing.

At the state level, the constitutional debt limits can best be described as miserly; in those states that set dollar limits on debt, none of the limits exceeds $2 million. Some are much lower: Rhode Island's constitution permits a state debt of only $50,000, and Nebraska's limit is $100,000. Provisions for indebtedness vary widely among states, but in general there are stringent limitations on borrowing that appear to be more than adequate to prevent politicians from plundering the taxpayer's purse. Moreover, there are constitutional as well as statutory bounds on operating deficits—more than half the states have legal provisions that require spending reductions if there is a shortfall in revenue; at least seven states go even further and constitutionally mandate that taxes be increased to offset any operating deficit.

In the railroad construction bonanza of the 1860s and 1870s state governments were largely prohibited from any involvement in such ventures. Local governments, however, were not burdened with such constraints, and local politicians were quick to recognize that rail service could determine whether a community thrived or even survived. To entice the railroads to provide service, municipalities would either guarantee the railroad's bonds to aid the company in raising capital or would employ the proceeds of a municipal bond issue to purchase

15

railroad stock. As one historian has observed, these ventures were a replay of the excesses of the state governments decades earlier:

> When much of this investment [in railroads], supposedly for community advancement, turned out to be a total loss there was widespread default and repudiation of municipal debt that plagued both municipalities and investors for many years. While a majority of state court decisions sustained such borrowing as being for a public purpose, the policy was widely repudiated by the people themselves. State after state amended its constitution to prohibit local governments from making gifts or loans of money, property, or credit to, or owning the stock of private corporations and undertakings.[9]

State restrictions on local government finance are still widespread. Generally, limits are imposed on borrowing based on a percentage of property values, although the requirements vary from state to state and different limits may be imposed on counties, municipalities, and school districts. At least 20 states make no provision for exceeding the limits, even by popular vote, although there are often "special cases." Kansas, for example, mandates that general obligation long-term debt incurred by counties cannot exceed one percent of "state equalized assessed value" of property except for debt undertaken for hospitals and for certain other "specified purposes."

The restrictions on general obligation borrowing by local governments are more rigorous than at the state level. Virtually every state has constitutional or statutory provisions that either limit the amount of debt to a fixed proportion of property values or require local referenda. Further, many states regulate by statute or constitutional provision the terms and conditions under which local borrowing must be undertaken.

The particulars of the borrowing restrictions at the state and local levels of government are not of major interest. The point is that various checks that have been instituted would seem to be more than adequate to assure the taxpayer that there is no cause for concern about the abuse of public financing. However, the taxpayer who sleeps soundly because of the security provided by constitutional and statutory protections on public debt is profoundly naive about the wiles of politicians and public employees. This statement should not be interpreted to mean that politicians and public employees are, as individuals, more devious and

---

[9]Lennox L. Moak and Albert M. Hillhouse, *Concepts and Practices in Local Government Finance* (Chicago: Municipal Finance Officers Association, 1975), p. 262. Also, see Albert M. Hillhouse, *Municipal Bonds: A Century of Experience* (New York: Prentice Hall, Inc., 1936), esp. chap. VII.

dishonest than individuals who work in the private sector. Neither public nor private sector employees are inherently "saints" or "sinners"; neither group has a monopoly on horns or halos. All individuals, regardless of the sector in which they work, serve their own private interests first and foremost. They engage in activities which enhance their prestige and income and avoid taking courses of action that produce undesirable consequences for their careers. The incentive structure in the public sector is vastly different from that in the private sector and, as a result, the means of obtaining rewards and avoiding punishment are vastly different.

The long-accepted and rarely challenged notion that politicians and public employees are "public servants" who seek only to serve the public interest is a myth, for it implies schizophrenic behavior by public employees. If an individual employed in the private sector accepts public-sector employment, he does not undergo a personality change that causes him to consider only the public interest when making decisions rather than his own interest. There is no doubt, however, that the perpetuation of the myth serves the politician's and the bureaucrat's purposes well, for what could be more self-serving and less public-spirited than challenging an action deemed essential to the well-being of the body politic? Thus, the myth provides those in the public sector an excellent foil which may be used to deflect criticism and to discredit critics. The myth must be destroyed and, with it, the naivete of the public that has long permitted politicians and bureaucrats to manage the public sector in a way that serves their own designs.

Politicians and public employees are professionals at developing and exploiting loopholes in the law and, despite the explicit checks and balances that have existed for decades, have found little difficulty in overcoming constitutional constraints and statutory restrictions on spending and borrowing.[10] Repeatedly, constraints have been placed on public expenditures at taxpayer insistence without much effect or even serious inconvenience to the politician. For example, in the 1920s, the state of Arizona placed limitations on the expenditures from county General Funds to restrict local spending. The solution for county poli-

---

[10]This should come as no surprise to the student of constitutional law. Bernard Siegan, in his recent book, *Economic Liberties and the Constitution* (Chicago: University of Chicago Press, 1980), documents how, for decades, legislatures have passed laws which effectively abolish many of the economic liberties embodied in the federal constitution. And, as Siegan illustrates, the Supreme Court has upheld most of these changes since the mid-1930s.

ticians was to create new funds not subject to the restriction and to ask for special exemptions for other funds from the state legislature:

> [E]xempt funds include the Road Fund, the Health Services Fund, the Public Works Reserve Fund, the Auto License Fund, the Federal Revenue Sharing Fund, the Anti-Recession Fiscal Assistance Fund, and various specific grants funds. In addition there are a whole host of exclusions, including air pollution, cemeteries and indigent health costs, war emergency, TB control, and superior court costs.[11]

Thus, when certain categories of expenditures are constrained, politicians merely redefine the categories. Very strict spending limitation provisions—whether constitutional or statutory—also have escape clauses which permit the expenditure ceiling to be bypassed, usually in "emergency" circumstances. Limits may be very ambiguous or difficult to interpret and, therefore, all but impossible to implement. One student of spending limitations has concluded:

> It is probably impossible to frame an amendment which cannot be evaded. Constitutions are made to be interpreted. . . .[12] All [the] problems of implementation arise from questions of interpretation. It is impossible to close every potential loophole or to foresee in detail all potential problems. Whether the limitation would be enforced would depend in the last resort not so much on its wording, but on the degree to which it hampers the objectives of those subject to it, the belief it engenders that it is beneficial in its results, and the willingness of those who apply it to abide by its spirit.[13]

The historical record clearly indicates that politicians have long had a proclivity for excessive borrowing and spending and, despite bad experiences with such excesses, have continued to seek ways to enhance their own interests with taxpayers bearing the burden. Thus, the recent tax revolt cannot be viewed as a one-time confrontation between taxpayers and politicians but a continuing skirmish which flares into the headlines from time to time. A survey of the more recent record indicates that the taxpayer may occasionally even win a battle, but the war is being lost.

---

[11]Naomi Caiden, "Problems in Implementing Government Expenditure Limitation," in Aaron Wildavsky, *How to Limit Government Spending* (Berkeley: University of California Press, 1980), appendix C, p. 150.

[12]Ibid., p. 158.

[13]Ibid., p. 162.

18

The Continuing Saga of the Tax Revolt

As discussed above, tax revolts have flared from time to time in response to the more blatant episodes of political profligacy. The most recent chapter of this continuing saga consists of the well-publicized "tax revolt of the '70s." As shown in Table 2, 32 states have imposed 54 different limitations on local government taxing and spending powers since 1970.[14] Eighteen initiatives were passed in 11 states during the period 1970–73, followed by only three in 1974 and 1975. But in 1975 the tax revolt began to ferment. Taxpayers approved only 29 percent of the total amount of state and local government bond referenda in that year compared to 64 percent in 1974.[15] Then from 1976 to 1980, 33 tax or spending limitation initiatives were implemented, including the infamous Proposition 13 in California in June of 1978. Thus, the taxpayer revolt of the 1970s appears to have begun in earnest in 1976, the 200th anniversary of the most famous taxpayer revolt of all, the American Revolution. Several states also placed limits on state taxing and spending during that time, and 30 state legislatures voted to convene a convention to add a balanced budget amendment to the federal constitution. The rapid growth of the underground private economy during the 1970s could be considered the ultimate stage of the tax revolt. Furthermore, one could argue that the electoral successes of Ronald Reagan and the Republicans in the Senate in 1980 were spawned by the tax revolt.

The most recent taxpayer revolt is clearly more than just a passing fad. The rash of constitutional and statutory limitations placed on government spending and taxing powers is the result of a deep-seated and widely espoused dissatisfaction by taxpayers with paying more and more of their incomes in taxes and getting less and less in return. Taxpayers have learned that the government solutions to society's problems proposed by reformers of the New Deal, the Fair Deal, the New Frontier, the Great Society, and so on have not been realized, and in many instances have exacerbated existing problems. Adding insult to injury, the bills for all these programs continue to come due, for once a government program is started, it quickly builds up a constit-

[14]The limits listed in Table 2 are self-explanatory except for "full disclosure," which requires local officials to warn taxpayers of property tax increases by advertising them, and by voting on them at public hearings. Also, note that 32 limitations existed prior to 1970.

[15]Advisory Commission on Intergovernmental Relations, *Significant Features of Fiscal Federalism: 1980–81* (Washington, D.C.: ACIR, 1981).

Table 2

STATE RESTRICTIONS ON LOCAL GOVERNMENT TAXING AND SPENDING

	Property Tax Rate Limit	Property Tax Levy Limit	General Revenue Limit	General Expenditure Limit	Limit on Assessment Increases	Full Disclosure	Total
Before 1970	29	3	0	0	0	0	32
1971	1	2	0	2	0	1	6
1972	3	1	0	0	0	0	4
1973	3	4	0	1	0	0	8
1974	1	0	0	0	0	1	2
1975	0	0	0	0	0	1	1
1976	1	3	0	1	0	1	6
1977	0	1	0	0	2	1	4
1978	2	3	0	0	1	0	6
1979	1	2	2	2	1	2	10
1980	3	2	0	1	1	0	7

SOURCE: Calculated from Advisory Commission on Intergovernmental Relations, *State Imposed Restrictions on Local Government Tax and Expenditure Powers* (Washington, D.C.: ACIR, 1981).

uency among bureaucrats, politicians, and beneficiary groups which will fight very hard against threats of budget cuts or abolition of the agency, regardless of whether the agency's goals are being achieved or not.

The rising burdens of taxation and inflation are good reasons for the American taxpayer's frustrations. The median-income family was actually poorer in 1981 than in 1971 after accounting for direct federal taxes and inflation. As shown in Table 3, real median family income was fully $427 less in 1981 than 10 years earlier. In addition to this, state and local taxes grew by over 25 percent in real terms during this period, making the taxpayer even worse off.

The Tax Foundation has developed one of the easiest ways to see the "tax bite" on the American taxpayer. Each year the Foundation computes "Tax Freedom Day," the day of the year on which the average

Table 3

MEDIAN FAMILY INCOMES BEFORE AND AFTER DIRECT FEDERAL
TAXES AND INFLATION
1971–1981

| Year | Median Family Income[a] | Direct Federal Taxes | | | After-Tax Income | |
		Income Tax[b]	Social Security	Total	Current Dollars	1971 Dollars[c]
1971	$10,314	$ 933	$ 406	$1,339	$ 8,975	$8,975
1972	11,152	982	468	1,450	9,702	9,392
1973	11,895	1,098	632	1,730	10,165	9,264
1974	13,004	1,267	761	2,028	10,976	9,014
1975	14,156	1,172	825	1,997	12,159	9,149
1976	15,016	1,388	878	2,266	12,750	9,071
1977	15,949	1,466	933	2,399	13,550	9,056
1978	17,318	1,717	1,048	2,765	14,553	9,034
1979	19,097	1,876	1,171	3,047	16,050	8,955
1980	20,900[d]	2,197	1,281	3,478	17,422	8,563
1981	23,700[d]	2,801[e]	1,576	4,377	19,323	8,548

[a]Median income for all families with one earner employed full-time, year-round.
[b]Married couple filing joint return, two children.
[c]Adjusted by Consumer Price Index of the Bureau of Labor Statistics.
[d]1980 and 1981 estimated by Tax Foundation.
[e]Assumes no change in current law.
SOURCE: Tax Foundation, *Monthly Tax Features,* June–July 1981.

worker can stop working for the government and start working to support himself and his family. In 1981, the average American spent 130 days working to pay taxes; Tax Freedom Day was May 10, after federal, state, and local governments had taken over 35 percent of the average worker's earnings.[16] As shown in Table 4, taxes take a greater proportion of the average worker's income than any other item or, in fact, than any other two items combined. In 1981 the worker on a 9-5:30 shift worked almost until lunch to satisfy the appetite of the tax collector.

American taxpayers are disgruntled not only over the amount of time they must spend working to pay their taxes, but also over the amount of time spent preparing their tax payments. The U.S. Tax Code is extraordinarily complicated, and its verbose language can confuse even the most determined taxpayer. It grew from just a few pages after World War II to over 1,200 pages by 1981. There are also over 3,000 pages of Treasury regulations, and the Federal Tax Case Law takes up

Table 4

TAX BITE IN THE EIGHT-HOUR DAY
FOR THE AVERAGE AMERICAN WORKER IN 1981

Item	Hours and Minutes	% of Time
Tax, Total	2 hours 49 minutes	35.2
Federal	1 hour 56 minutes	24.2
State and Local	53 minutes	11.0
Housing and Household Operation	1 hour 28 minutes	18.3
Food and Beverages	1 hour 4 minutes	13.3
Transportation	43 minutes	9.0
Medical Care	29 minutes	6.0
Clothing	22 minutes	4.5
Recreation	19 minutes	4.0
All other*	46 minutes	9.5
TOTAL	8 hours	

*"All other" includes expenditures for items such as personal care, personal business, private education, and savings.

SOURCE: Tax Foundation, *Monthly Tax Features*, April 1981.

[16]Tax Foundation, *Monthly Tax Features*, April 1981. This compares to a February 14 Tax Freedom Day in 1930.

22

50 feet of shelf space.[17] Even the definition of "employment" comprises over 1,000 words, 19 semicolons, and 42 parentheses.[18] Some of the sentences in the Tax Code are so long that they are virtually indecipherable. Some examples are Section 170 (b)(i)(A), 379 words; Section 6651 (a), 385 words; and Section 7701 (a)(19), 506 words! Even some of the shorter sentences in the Code are unintelligible. For example, the last sentence of Section 509 (a) states that

> For purposes of paragraph (3), an organization described in paragraph (2) shall be deemed to include an organization described in Section 501 (c)(4), (5), or (6) which would be described in Paragraph (2) if it were an organization described in Section 501 (c)(3).[19]

Things are not much simpler at the state or local level. Local governments collect real and personal property taxes, amusement taxes, wage taxes, hotel and restaurant taxes, utility taxes, and fees of every kind. At the state level, there are income taxes, sales taxes, taxes on gasoline, liquor, cigarettes, unemployment taxes, and other levies that are steadily proliferating. The complexity of local taxation is exemplified by the number of tax reports required of a sole proprietor of a business being established in the city of New York. He is liable for more than 20 different taxes or statements, and if two or more staff are employed, he must file at least 37 separate tax reports each year,[20] including six with the city, 17 with the federal government, and 14 with the state.

Obviously, the tax laws are too cumbersome for the average (or above average) American to understand. A recent IRS survey found that over 44 million Americans, worried over being "caught" in a mistake, had someone else—lawyers, tax accountants—prepare their 1978 tax returns for them.[21] Even the taxpayer who takes the time to learn the tax laws and challenges the IRS in tax court is bound to be greatly frustrated. As of July 1982 the backlog of cases exceeded 48,000 and was growing, and taxpayers in some areas had to wait as long as a year and a half for their cases to come to trial.[22] Because of the thousands of special exemptions and deductions in the tax code, many also see the system

---

[17]Dan Bawley, *The Subterranean Economy* (New York: McGraw-Hill, 1982), p. 41.
[18]Ibid.
[19]Ibid., p. 42.
[20]Ibid., p. 120.
[21]S. Aitken and L. Bonneville, "A General Taxpayer Opinion Survey," Study by CSR, Inc., Washington, D.C., for the Office of Planning and Research, IRS, March 1980.
[22]"Tax Report," *Wall Street Journal,* June 23, 1981, p. 1.

as inherently "unfair," in that many wealthy individuals are able to escape the grasp of the tax collector through various loopholes.[23] "Voluntary compliance" has long been the phrase used to describe the collection methods of the federal income tax: Taxpayers report their own income and deductions and compute their own tax liability. The existence and rapid expansion of the underground economy is direct evidence that voluntary compliance is beginning to crumble. As wealthy taxpayers take advantage of various shelters to reduce their taxes, lower-income individuals resent paying their share of the total tax bill and avoid doing so by not filing returns or by underreporting income. Tax evasion feeds upon itself in the sense that as the practice becomes more widespread, it loses its stigma and becomes a socially accepted practice. Tax collection in both France and Italy has deteriorated to this point, to name only two cases. The public sector in the United States is now finding its ability to collect taxes impaired and, unless major changes are made in the tax codes to reduce complexity and increase the perceived equity of the system, the situation is destined to get much worse rather than better. The taxpayer's pocket is not a bottomless pit nor is his patience inexhaustible.

The Indirect Costs of Government

The average worker turns over more than a third of his income to various levels of government in taxes, but that is only part of the burden of government. Government imposes many other costs on the taxpayer that are difficult to measure, but are very real. The prices paid for goods and services have, in many cases, risen dramatically because of the regulatory activities of government. As one example, it is estimated that because of federal regulations imposed between 1968 and 1978, the average cost of a new car has been pushed up by $665.87.[24] Since approximately 10 million new cars and trucks are purchased each year, government regulations cost car purchasers about $6.7 billion annually.

Over the past 20 years, dozens of regulatory programs have been introduced at the federal level. The Federal Register has mushroomed from 20,000 pages of regulations in 1970 to over 77,000 pages in 1979.

---

[23]Nearly everyone has heard of millionaires who (legally) pay no taxes, but the fact of the matter is that the highest 50 percent of income-earners paid 93.5 percent of federal taxes in 1978; the highest 25 percent paid 73.8 percent; the highest 10 percent paid 49.7 percent; and these ratios are all rising. See Tax Foundation, *Monthly Tax Features*, June-July 1980, p. 3.

[24]Murray Weidenbaum, *The Future of Business Regulation* (New York: Amacom Books, 1979), p. 13.

The federal government has dictated the shape of toilet seats, the size of knotholes permissible in wood to build ladders, and the way in which stepladders may be climbed. Although the contents of many regulations may be comic, the price tag to American consumers is not. One carefully developed, conservative estimate placed the cost of federal regulation of businesses at over $102 billion in 1979—approximately $500 per capita.[25] A similar expansion of regulatory activity has also taken place at the state and local levels of government and, combined with federal regulation, has severely impaired the vitality of American industry and contributed to unemployment.

Regulation has traditionally been justified as a means of protecting "the public interest," however defined. But despite these claims, a large number of economic studies have shown that many regulations are not only costly but are also ineffective. For example, many of the automobile regulations are related to safety, yet a study done at the University of Chicago showed that these safety devices have no effect whatever in reducing death rates from automobile accidents since they don't take into account the principal cause of automobile fatalities— the drunk driver. The Occupational Safety and Health Administration supposedly was established to reduce hazards to workers on the job. Yet a study reported that the agency's enforcement policies have not had any direct impact on job hazards.[26] The regulation of new drugs has sharply reduced the rates of innovation and introduction of effective new drugs, whereas in Great Britain and many other countries where the drug environment is less restrictive there have been marked benefits from new drugs that have not been introduced in the U.S.[27] These studies are just a few among hundreds conducted in the past two decades. They indicate why so many economists in particular and taxpayers in general are critical of government regulation. Many of the studies have been published in the *Journal of Law and Economics* whose editor, Ronald Coase, said:

> [T]here have been more serious studies made of government regulation of industry in the last fifteen years or so, particularly in the United States, than in the whole preceding period. These studies have been both quantitative and nonquantitative. . . . The main lesson to be

[25]Ibid.

[26]W.K. Viscusi, "The Impact of Occupational Safety and Health Regulation," *Bell Journal of Economics*, Spring 1979, p. 136.

[27]Sam Peltzman, *Regulation of Pharmaceutical Innovation: The 1962 Amendments* (Washington, D.C.: American Enterprise Institute, 1974).

25

drawn from these studies is clear: they all tend to suggest that the regulation is either ineffective or that when it has a noticeable impact, on balance the effect is bad, so that consumers obtain a worse product or a higher-priced product or both as a result of the regulation. Indeed, this result is found so uniformly as to create a puzzle: one would expect to find, in all these studies, at least some government programs that do more good than harm.[28]

Despite the "public interest" rhetoric, it is also evident that much economic regulation serves various special interests at the expense of the general public. Trucking regulation has maintained cartel pricing arrangements for the benefit of trucking firms and the Teamsters Union; airline regulation restricted entry into the airline industry; occupational licensing restricts entry into various professions from fortune-telling to the practice of medicine, and so on.

Another indirect cost of regulation which has helped to foster an anti-government spirit in the past decade is government red tape. As of June 1972 the Office of Management and Budget reported that federal agencies (excluding the IRS) used 5,567 forms that generate 418 million responses—about two for every man, woman, and child in the country. The costs and frustrations involved in federal paperwork are enormous. Consider the following statement from the *Final Summary Report* of the U.S. Commission on Federal Paperwork issued in October 1977:

> The total costs of federal paperwork are difficult to determine; but, as best we can estimate, more than $100 billion a year, or about $500 for each person in this country, is spent on federal paperwork. Our estimates of costs to some major segments of society are:
>
> *The federal government: $43 billion per year
> *Private industry: $25 to 32 billion per year
> *State and local government: $5 to 9 billion per year
> *Individuals: $8.7 billion per year
> *Farmers: $350 million per year
> *Labor Organizations: $75 million per year[29]

The paperwork burden imposes heavy costs on small businesses in particular, which can ill afford to spend the time, effort, and money required to comply with the bureaucracy's seemingly insatiable desire for paperwork, much of which is redundant or just ignored.

[28]Ronald Coase, "Economists and Public Policy," in J.F. Weston, *Large Corporations in a Changing Society* (New York: New York University Press, 1975), pp. 182–84.

[29]U.S. Commission on Federal Paperwork, *Final Summary Report* (Washington, D.C.: U.S. Government Printing Office, 1977), p. 5.

It is clear that if the indirect costs of government regulation are added to the direct costs of taxation, Tax Freedom Day would come much later than May 10.

Government Failure and the Alienated Voter

The failures of government regulation have been replicated by failures of various government agencies to deal with problems such as housing, poverty, energy crises, low-quality primary and secondary education, and so on, despite the expenditure of hundreds of billions of dollars. It appears that taxpayers are frustrated not only with the continual tax drain on their incomes, but also with the fact that they seem to be getting so little for their tax dollars.

For example, since President Lyndon Johnson declared "war on poverty" in 1964, the federal government has spent more than $30 billion on poverty programs, which must be judged abject failures. This sum, along with all the other governmental "social welfare" programs, is enough to lift every man, woman and child out of poverty three times over. Despite all these well-intentioned efforts, an estimated 29 million Americans remain below the official poverty level.[30] The evidence indicates that much of the anti-poverty money has not benefited the poor, but has generated much affluence among those employed in the "poverty industry"—government bureaucrats, college professors, consultants, special interest groups, lobbyists, and research firms, among others. Former Treasury Secretary William Simon recently calculated that if all the money spent by federal, state, and local governments were simply given to those below the poverty level, each family of four below the poverty line would receive approximately $40,000 annually!

Things are not much different in other areas in which the federal government has intervened, most notably energy and housing. The Department of Energy admits to having had no favorable effect on energy problems despite employing over 20,000 people and spending more than $10 billion annually by 1979.[31] The Department of Housing and Urban Development (HUD) has spent more than $76 billion since 1965 in pursuit of its official objective of "decent housing for every American," yet slums abound in the nation's cities and rural areas.

---

[30]D. Lambro, *Fat City: How Washington Wastes Your Taxes* (South Bend, Ind.: Regnery/Gateway, Inc., 1980), p. 63.

[31]In fact, a very strong case can be made that the Department of Energy has been a major *cause* of our energy problems, especially in light of its ill-fated price control and entitlement programs.

According to the government, HUD has financed about one million housing units, mostly apartments, for the poor. But one researcher has found that if HUD's $76 billion were actually spent on housing for the poor, it could have purchased more than 1.5 million $50,000 single-family homes at 1979 prices.[32] Much of the money, at least $10 billion, has gone for research projects, the services of consulting firms, construction of lavish upper-income communities, "model" cities, many of which have turned into slums and gone bankrupt, public relations promotions on behalf of HUD itself, and grants to municipalities and organizations which have nothing to do with housing for the poor.[33]

At the state and local levels of government, where public spending and taxation is more visible than at the federal level, performance has been poor, to say the least, despite a rate of expenditure growth which has exceeded that of the federal government's during the past two decades. The tax revolt of the '70s, symbolized by Proposition 13, seems to have been most vocal at the local level of government where, despite rising property taxes,[34] crime rates continue to soar, roads are full of potholes, and educational achievement at the primary and secondary levels has been on the decline for years. The major component of local government spending—education—provides a case in point. As shown in Table 5, public school enrollment increased from 1961 through 1972, then began to decline. Revenues, however, continued to rise. Between academic years 1975–76 and 1977–78, total enrollment declined by more than one million students while spending rose by over $10 billion, only a small part of which can be attributed to inflation.

It is possible, of course, that spending more money on fewer students can be explained in terms of higher quality education, but the evidence indicates that exactly the opposite is true. Despite a threefold increase in spending *per student* from 1961 to 1978, the average Scholastic Aptitude Test score on the verbal exam was 9.3 percent *lower* in 1978 than in 1961, and the average math score dropped six percent during that time. Public education has deteriorated to such a point that some states now require students to pass basic literacy exams before graduating from high school.

Growing taxpayer frustration and disillusionment with government

[32]Lambro, p. 121.

[33]Ibid.

[34]General revenues of local governments tripled between 1969 and 1979, from $72 to $212 billion. This was the steepest rate of growth of local revenue of any decade on record. See Tax Foundation, *Monthly Tax Features*, June–July 1981, p. 4.

Table 5

PUBLIC SCHOOL ENROLLMENT, REVENUE, AND REVENUE PER STUDENT, SELECTED YEARS, 1961–1978

School Year	Enrollment (thousands)	Revenue (millions)	$ Per Student	Scholastic Aptitude Test Verbal	Scholastic Aptitude Test Quantitative
1961–62	37,464	17,527.7	468	468	498
1963–64	40,187	20,420.0	500	475	498
1965–66	42,173	25,356.9	601	471	496
1967–68	43,891	31,903.1	727	466	494
1969–70	45,619	40,266.9	883	460	488
1971–72	46,081	50,003.7	1,085	453	484
1972–73	45,744	52,117.9	1,139	445	481
1973–74	45,429	58,230.9	1,282	444	480
1974–75	45,053	61,099.6	1,356	434	472
1975–76	44,791	70,802.8	1,580	431	472
1977–78	43,731	80,925.0	1,851	429	468

SOURCE: Tax Foundation, *Facts and Figures on Government Finance, 1979* (Washington, D.C.: Tax Foundation, 1979), pp. 255, 257.

has been clearly revealed in a series of national surveys conducted between 1964 and 1976 by the Center for Political Studies at the University of Michigan. These show a steady erosion in the public's trust in government.[35] In 1976, 62 percent of Americans believed that government could be trusted "to do what is right" for them *only some* rather than most of the time; in 1964 the figure was 22 percent. More and more Americans are viewing government as being too powerful and extremely wasteful. In 1976, 50 percent of the public believed that government had grown too powerful, compared to 31 percent in 1964. The proportion of people believing that government wastes "a lot" of their tax money increased from 46 percent in 1964 to 74 percent in 1976. These attitudes are widespread in all sectors of society and there is remarkably little variation in the skeptical view of government among the young, middle-aged, and elderly, between the poor and those who are well-off, liberals and conservatives, and whites and nonwhites.

The message is clear: Taxpayers believe that they are paying too

[35]Jacob Citrin, "The Alienated Voter," *Taxing and Spending,* October–November 1978, pp. 7–11.

much and getting too little from government and, in order to force politicians to be more responsible and cost-conscious, are trying to impose constitutional and statutory limitations on taxes, spending, and borrowing. So deep is the discontent among citizens that disgruntled taxpayers have begun to vent their anger by bodily attacking local government employees. As a result, some local civil servants are demanding "combat pay" for work "in the front lines of the municipal infantry," and union contracts in New York City now provide for 18 months of leave with full pay after an assault.[36]

Has the tax revolt been effective? A *New York Times* editorial has asserted that the tide is finally turning; state and local government spending since 1978 is actually expected to decline.[37] A statistical study of the effects of tax and spending limitations imposed on local governments conducted by the Advisory Commission on Intergovernmental Relations concluded that they have indeed been successful.[38] Many social scientists now routinely assume that tax and spending limitations put money into the taxpayers' pockets and promote efficiency and responsiveness in government.[39] In addition, there are many who place great faith in the ability of a balanced budget amendment to the Constitution to produce a greater degree of economic stability and to constrain inflation. The Reagan administration claims to be firmly committed to both a balanced budget and spending limitations at the federal level.

One would think that with more than two centuries of experience with constitutional and statutory restrictions on government powers, there would be a solid basis for such optimism. It appears, however, that no one has even examined the historical record on the success or failure of taxing, spending, and borrowing limitations. For over three-quarters of a century, state and local governments have routinely evaded all restrictions on their financial independence by the simple expedient of moving large segments of the public sector off-budget. Off-budget spending at the federal level is also gaining momentum. What is needed is a better understanding of how governments respond to these limi-

[36]Jeffrey Sheler, "The New Incivility Toward Civil Servants," *U.S. News & World Report*, July 27, 1981, pp. 56–57.

[37]Rudolph Penner, "Why Local Spending is Finally Slowing," *New York Times*, December 7, 1980, p. D-2.

[38]Advisory Commission on Intergovernmental Relations, *State Limitations on Local Taxes and Expenditures* (Washington, D.C.: ACIR, 1977).

[39]For example, see M. Menchilk, "Fiscal Limitation Fever: Who Gets Hurt?" *Journal Of Contemporary Studies*, Winter 1981, pp. 67–80.

tations so that we can accurately assess our options for effectively reducing the size and growth of government. These issues are developed more fully in later chapters.

Summary

History shows that politicians have long had a proclivity for excessive borrowing and spending and, despite bad experiences with such excesses, proceed along the same path and continue to invent new ways to enhance their own interests at the expense of the public's interests. Taxpayer revolts against such political profligacy are part and parcel of American political history, and have been even since the nation's founders rebelled against the political abuses imposed upon them by the British government. Tax revolts have flared throughout the past two centuries in response to the more blatant episodes of political abuse, and the current tax revolt is certainly one of the strongest, having established dozens of constitutional and statutory constraints on the spending and taxing powers of state and local governments, and pressured the federal government to reduce the growth of spending and taxation and return to the classical economic philosophy of budgetary balance. American taxpayers are clearly fed up with paying ever-increasing proportions of their income in taxes and getting less and less in return.

As a result of the most recent tax revolt, many citizens are hopeful that constitutional and statutory constraints on taxing and spending, or the threat of such constraints, will begin to curtail the political plundering of the taxpayer's purse. But politicians who are wily enough to ignore taxpayer's preferences to the extent that a taxpayer revolt is spawned can also be expected to ignore any further constraints imposed on their behavior by the citizenry.

III. The Political Economy of Off-Budget Enterprise

Fiscal Constraint and the Politician

On the surface, it would seem that tax revolts and fiscal constraints in the form of statutory or constitutional restrictions on taxation, spending, or debt pose major problems for ambitious politicians. After all, fiscal limitations of any sort restrict the freedom of action of policymakers in the public sector to pursue their own political goals. When public opinion supports constitutional or statutory limits on taxes, expenditures, and borrowing by government, the politician who ignores the will of the voter does so at his own peril. Elected officials are also aware that a favorable impression can be made on voters by advocating the reduction in the size and scope of government and the improvement in the efficiency of the public sector. Opinion polls have shown for years that there is a widespread belief that government is "too big" and "wasteful." The Reagan administration plays on such sentiments in advocating a balanced budget amendment to the constitution, despite the fact that the budgets proposed by the administration contain deficits that are enormous by historical standards. Of course, the proposed amendment would not take effect until Reagan is out of the White House so that the problem of budget balancing is passed to the President's successor while the current administration collects the political benefits.

For elected officials, however, continued expansion of the public sector and the associated patronage which can be dispensed to supporters are key elements of success. Ideally, the politician would like to preach fiscal conservatism to his constituents while simultaneously increasing the size and scope of the public sector. Off-budget enterprises, as explained in detail below, permit politicians to perform this feat. As discussed in Chapter II, spending limitations can be avoided by redefining categories of expenditure, and tax limitations can be avoided with user fees. Limitations on debt, however, are more difficult to manipulate, for it is not as easy to disguise debt. Throughout history lenders have been notoriously suspicious of borrowers. Politicians, however, are crafty and, although constraints on spending, taxing, and borrowing have long existed for state and local governments, resourceful elected officials have successfully side-stepped virtually all restrictions on their financial independence.

The evasion of restrictions on public debt required a more novel approach than was the case with taxes and expenditures, but the solution developed was disarmingly simple: separate corporate entities created by state and local governments which could issue bonds that were not subject to the legal restrictions on public debt. These entities masquerade under a variety of guises; they are called districts, boards, authorities, agencies, commissions, corporations, and trusts. Regardless of their title, an essential feature of all these organizations is that their financial activities do not appear in the budget of the government unit or units that created them. Thus, politicians have been able to make part of the public sector simply disappear by forming separate entities—off-budget enterprises (OBEs)—to conduct borrowing and spending activities.

It is important to understand how OBEs operate in general and how politicians benefit from their existence, in particular, because off-budget operations provide benefits to elected officials which could not be obtained from an on-budget operation *even if debt limits did not exist.* The mechanics of the OBE are explored in the following fashion: First, the historical roots of the OBE device are briefly discussed; second, some data are presented on the size and scope of off-budget activities nationwide; third, the roles of the principal actors involved in the OBE drama and their motivations are explored in order to identify the goals and objectives of the various special-interest groups that inevitably arise whenever such an entity is created; finally, the rationales provided to the public for off-budget agencies are critically examined in order to demonstrate that these justifications lack substance and raise many significant issues about whether off-budget finance is appropriate.

A Historical Overview of Off-Budget Enterprise

The historical roots of off-budget organizations can be traced back at least as far as early 18th century England when toll bridges were financed by "revenue bonds." Bonds were issued to pay for the construction of toll bridges, and toll revenues were pledged to repay the principal and interest on the bonds. One distinguishing characteristic of OBEs is that their operations, at least in theory, are not financed from taxes but from revenues generated by their activities. Because the taxpayer is not deemed to be liable for the financial obligations of OBEs, voter approval

34

is not required for the debt issued by such organizations and, more importantly, debt restrictions do not apply. In the U.S., revenue bonds were first issued by the city of Spokane, Washington, in 1895.[1] No great feat of logic was required to establish a separate corporate entity to issue bonds and, simultaneously, to escape the borrowing restrictions that had been imposed on the unit of government that had created the corporation.

The first attempt at off-budget financing occurred at the close of the 19th century in Maine. The city of Waterville wanted to build a new city hall and established the Waterville New City Hall Commission in 1898 to finance the construction. The city transferred a lot to the Commission for the construction site, and the Commission hired a contractor. The contractor was to be paid from the proceeds of a bond offering by the Commission and debt service on the bonds was to be provided from rent for the building, which the city would pay to the Commission from taxes. The act creating the Commission was held unconstitutional in 1898 because the court ruled that the arrangement was a disguised mortgage that violated the debt limitation imposed on the city by the Maine constitution. Ultimately, the taxpayers were responsible for the debt on the proposed city hall so that borrowing restrictions were deemed applicable by the court. Not dismayed, Waterville politicians regrouped and tried again to evade the debt limits, but chose a different tack. In 1899, the Kennebec Water District was formed as a separate corporation to supply water to the city. The District was to issue its own bonds in order to purchase the private water companies operating in the area, and revenues from providing water service were to be used to pay interest and retire the debt. Because the operations of the water authority were not to be financed by taxes, but from revenues from water service, the Kennebec Water District received judicial approval. The Supreme Judicial Court of Maine held that the debt created was not in fact a debt of the city, and the District's debt was legal because the constitutional limitations on borrowing did not apply to a district established as a separate corporation.[2] Had the constitutional debt limit been applied to the Water District itself, the city of Waterville would have still been far ahead because the debt limit would have been effectively doubled. By superimposing separate corporations on a polit-

[1] D. Schlosser, C. Hoffman, A. Bauer, and G. Coleman, *Municipal Authorities in Pennsylvania* (Harrisburg, Pa: State of Pennsylvania Department of Community Affairs, 1977), p. 2.

[2] C. Robert Morris, "Evading Debt Limitations With Public Building Authorities: The Costly Subversion of State Constitutions," *Yale Law Journal* 68 (December 1958): 34–45.

ical jurisdiction, politicians could effectively multiply the debt limit, even if the debt limit is applied to each corporation. A major loophole had been opened which legally permitted politicians to bypass constitutional restrictions on debt by the simple expedient of chartering public corporations. Thus, at the turn of the century legal percedent had been established for off-budget operations by government in Maine and, as the American political maxim contends, "As Maine goes, so goes the nation." Off-budget enterprise had arrived on the American political scene.

The form of off-budget enterprise known as the "public authority" may be viewed as a creation of Congress, for the Port Authority of New York and New Jersey, established by federal law in 1921, became the prototype for virtually all of the public authorities in the U.S. The Port Authority was created to halt the bickering between the states of New York and New Jersey that had surrounded the operations of the harbor at the mouth of the Hudson River for more than a century. The boundaries of the two states had been arbitrarily drawn in the middle of the river and each state attempted to regulate its part of the harbor. Duplication of facilities and operations resulted, and during World War I the shipment of materials was delayed by the wrangling over which state controlled what portions of the port's operations. Because the federal constitution (Article I, paragraph 10, clause 3) prohibited any state from entering into an agreement or compact with any other state without the consent of Congress, a commission appointed by the governors of New York and New Jersey to study and resolve the problems of the port proposed the development of an interstate authority. (The title of "authority" was borrowed from then-operating Port of London Authority which performed similar functions.) Congress approved, and the nation's most renowed public authority came into existence.

Although the legal precedent for off-budget enterprise was established by the turn of the century and the Port Authority provided a prototype for state and local governments to follow, there was not widespread adoption of the concept until the 1930s when the federal government actively encouraged all units of government to go off-budget on an unprecedented scale. During the 1930s, public works were viewed as a cure for the economic ills of the Great Depression. The federal government provided grants-in-aid to state and local governments, but the grants covered only a portion of the total cost—the grantee government had to provide matching funds. All levels of government were in financial difficulties, if not in default, and could not avail themselves of the federal grants-in-aid; matching funds were not available. President Roosevelt wished to preserve the tradition of matching grants and, in order to do so, agreed to lend state and local governments their matching share, but a hitch developed. Financially strapped state and local governments had already borrowed to the limits permitted by constitutional and statutory restrictions and could not legally accept the federal loans. In December 1934, Roosevelt wrote to the governor of each state effectively suggesting the establishment of public corporations not subject to the debt limits so that the loans could be made and "economic recovery" could proceed expeditiously.[3] Undoubtedly, this action greatly spurred the development of off-budget enterprises.

This incident is not unique, for federal sponsorship of off-budget operations has continued over time and has been nonpartisan. In 1955, President Eisenhower actively advocated federal legislation to encourage local governments to create off-budget school building authorities that could ignore restrictive debt limits in order to build schools and undertake a wide range of activities, as discussed in greater detail in Chapter V. Federal government prodding and the promise of various forms of largesse from the national Treasury has contributed significantly to the explosive growth of OBEs at all levels of government.

The Growth of Off-Budget Activity

Unfortunately, it is simply impossible to obtain data on OBEs. Most states do not keep statistics on the number of corporations established by local governments. Indeed, for politicians, an important part of the intrinsic appeal of the OBE device is that its operations are not publicized. In almost every state, OBEs can be established by local governments without the consent of the legislature (Maine and New York are exceptions). To collect data from the thousands of counties, municipalities, townships, and boroughs throughout the U.S. would be very difficult and costly, if not impossible. One point may be made with certainty: There are thousands of OBEs throughout the nation engaging in a bewildering variety of activities. In Pennsylvania alone, there were 2,456 municipal authorities in operation as of July 1976, and collectively these OBEs had almost $5 billion in debt outstanding.[4]

Since 1950, the federal government has collected data related to off-budget operations of government, but for purposes here, these data

[3]D. Foley, "Revenue Financing of Public Enterprises," *Michigan Law Review* 35 (1936): 5–6.

[4]Schlosser, et. al.

are by no means either comprehensive or accurate. Not all OBEs are included, but information is included on a specific type of off-budget device—the "special district." Special districts differ from the OBE considered in this study in that they have taxing powers and may have elected directors rather than directors who are political appointees. Our concern is with organizational units that do not have taxing powers and have non-elected boards of directors. Aside from these two considerations, the differences between public authorities and special districts are relatively minor and involve far more form than substance, although the Census Bureau data confuse the issue by referring to OBEs and special districts as "special districts."

Special districts often are formed by two or more units of government whereas a "narrowly defined" OBE is typically established by a single political entity. In the state of California, for example, special districts have been created to control and distribute water supplies; school districts were also common throughout the U.S. In any case, census data provide some insights into the off-budget activities of state and local governments, despite the limitations.

Table 6 shows that between 1952 and 1962 the total number of OBEs rose by nearly 50 percent. Thereafter, the rate of growth slowed, but the total number increased so that by 1977 almost 26,000 of these entities were operating throughout the nation. In the quarter-century between 1952 and 1977, the number of quasi-public corporations more than doubled. The reduction in the percentage growth rate can be attributed, in part, to the fact that in the mid-1960s, federal programs began to

Table 6

NUMBER OF OFF-BUDGET ENTERPRISES IN THE U.S.
(INCLUDING SPECIAL DISTRICTS)
SELECTED YEARS, 1952–1977

Year	Number	% Increase from Preceding Reported Year
1952	12,339	—
1962	18,322	48.5
1967	21,264	16.1
1972	23,885	12.3
1977	25,962	8.7

SOURCE: U.S. Department of Commerce, Bureau of the Census, *Census of Governments*, various volumes.

emphasize grants to units of general government rather than to off-budget entities. Also, in 1972, the State and Local Fiscal Assistance Act was passed to provide for federal revenue sharing, with funds distributed to general-purpose governments.

Table 7 lists activities carried out by single-purpose and multiple-function off-budget enterprises. Obviously these organizations manage and control many sectors of public activity. It is important to note that many of the functions listed in Table 7 are also conducted by private firms, e.g., health care, hospitals, cemeteries, fire protection, housing, water supply, electric power generation, gas supply, and transit. Thus, the private sector is reduced as public enterprise proliferates. Although it may appear that, for some functions, there has been a decrease in the number of off-budget entities (highways, soil conservation, and other natural resources) over time, this does not mean that there has been a move to place these activities back "on-budget." Instead, one or more quasi-public corporations have merged into a single entity, which remains off-budget.

In theory, some off-budget enterprises should cease to exist after a specific period of time—these are "lease-back" enterprises which are usually designated as "authorities." Under a lease-back arrangement, an off-budget entity is created to issue bonds to finance a particular project such as the construction of a school building or the purchase of land for a cemetery. The authority then leases back the facility to the unit of government which created it and the project is operated by the government. The lease specifies an annual rental that is sufficient to pay off the outstanding bonds with interest, and the term of the lease coincides with the period that the bonds are outstanding. Once the bondholders have been reimbursed, ownership of the project is given to the public sector. The rationale for a lease-back authority then disappears, for the lease-back authority is solely a financial device for avoiding debt limits or for seeking voter approval to incur debt. The creation of any off-budget entity, however, simultaneously creates a powerful set of interest groups that benefit not only from its existence, but also from the continued expansion of its activities. Once created, powerful forces come into play to encourage off-budget enterprise to grow and undertake additional activities, as we shall see later. Thus, few lease-backs ever go out of existence, but actively seek ways to increase the number of projects in which they are involved.

In contrast to a lease-back entity, an operating authority assumes total responsibility for a project. The operating authority issues bonds to finance capital and operating costs, and bondholders are, at least in

Table 7

NUMBER OF OFF-BUDGET ENTITIES, BY FUNCTION
1962, 1967, 1972, AND 1977

Function	Number				% Change, 1962–1977
	1962	1967	1972	1977	
Single-function entities					
Cemeteries	1,283	1,397	1,496	1,615	25.9
School buildings	915	956	1,085	1,020	11.5
Fire protection	3,229	3,665	3,872	4,187	29.7
Highways	786	774	698	652	−17.0
Health	231	234	257	350	51.5
Hospitals	418	537	655	715	71.0
Housing and urban renewal	1,099	2,565	2,270	2,408	119.1
Libraries	349	410	498	586	67.9
Drainage	2,240	2,293	2,292	2,255	0.7
Flood control	500	662	677	681	36.2
Irrigation and water conservation	781	904	966	934	19.6
Soil conservation	2,461	2,572	2,564	2,432	−1.2
Other natural resources	309	209	231	294	−4.8
Parks and recreation	488	623	749	829	69.9
Sewers	937	1,233	1,406	1,610	71.8
Water supply	1,502	2,140	2,323	2,480	65.1
Electric power	76	75	74	82	7.9
Gas supply	30	37	48	46	53.3
Transit	10	14	33	96	860.0
Other	488	622	889	971	99.0
Multiple-function entities					
Sewer and water supply	13	298	629	1,065	671.7
Natural resources and water supply	56	45	67	71	26.8
Other	120	110	207	584	386.7

SOURCE: U.S. Department of Commerce, Bureau of the Census, *1977 Census of Governments*, Vol. 1, *Governmental Organization*, part 1, table 12.

theory, repaid from revenues generated by user fees. It is not uncommon, however, for the unit of government creating the authority or some other level of government to subsidize or provide grants to support the activities of an operating authority. Because the operating authority can be totally independent of government, provided its revenues are sufficient to cover its financial operations, the managers of operating authorities have far greater discretion than those involved in lease-backs. Operating authorities undertake such activities as sewer services, water and gas supply, and airport operations, to name a few.

The greatest growth in the number of single-function, off-budget entities has been in the areas of transit, housing, and urban renewal. These activities have three characteristics in common: (1) federal government funds have been very generous under a variety of aid programs; (2) local government performance in achieving positive results in these areas borders on the abysmal; and (3) the taxpayer, given the opportunity to vote on financing for such programs has repeatedly expressed an unwillingness to approve debt finance for such activities. Growth has also been very rapid in the "other" category for both single- and multiple-function enterprises. The "other" designation covers a multitude of sins. As examples, the state of New York, under Rockefeller's leadership, innovatively instituted a horse-breeding authority as well as an off-budget space development agency. One can only surmise the reaction taxpayers would give such schemes if financed on-budget. The apparent popularity of water and sewer supply corporations, which increased in number by 672 percent between 1962 and 1977, can be attributed largely to the efforts of the federal Environmental Protection Agency in urging construction of water treatment facilities.

The historical record reveals that the primary attraction of off-budget entities was the evasion of restrictive limitations on government borrowing. Data on indebtedness indicate that this goal has been achieved with a vengeance. Table 8 contains, for selected fiscal years, the level of gross long-term debt of state governments by type. "Full faith and credit" debt is approved by voters in a referendum and, should the need arise, taxes are increased to ensure payment of principal and interest. In contrast, off-budget enterprises issue debt that is "nonguaranteed" in the sense that there is no absolute assurance enforceable in court that repayment will be forthcoming from tax increases. Even in 1960, nonguaranteed debt accounted for just over one-half of total outstanding long-term state debt, indicating that the off-budget enterprise has long been a widely accepted device for state borrowing with-

Table 8

State Gross Long-Term Debt Outstanding by Type End of Selected Fiscal Years, 1960–1978 (millions of dollars)

Year	Total	Full Faith and Credit		Nonguaranteed	
		Amount	Percent of Total	Amount	Percent of Total
1960	18,128	8,912	49.2	9,216	50.8
1962	21,612	10,313	47.7	11,300	52.3
1964	24,401	11,147	45.7	13,254	54.3
1965	26,235	11,819	45.1	14,415	54.9
1966	28,504	12,709	44.6	15,795	55.4
1967	31,185	13,558	43.5	17,627	56.5
1968	33,618	14,698	43.7	18,920	56.3
1969	36,906	16,183	43.8	20,724	56.2
1970	38,903	17,736	45.6	21,167	54.4
1971	44,321	21,502	48.5	22,819	51.5
1972	50,542	25,228	49.9	25,314	50.1
1973	55,397	28,139	50.8	27,258	49.2
1974	61,697	30,855	50.0	30,842	50.0
1975	67,548	33,736	49.9	33,812	50.1
1976	78,814	38,842	49.3	39,972	50.7
1977	87,184	42,913	49.2	44,271	50.8
1978	109,450	48,286	44.1	61,164	55.9

Source: Tax Foundation, *Facts and Figures on Government Finance* (Washington, D.C.: Tax Foundation, Inc., 1979), p. 221.

out the difficulties associated with convincing often recalcitrant voters that the debt was desirable. By 1978, total long-term state debt outstanding exceeded $109 billion, a rise of more than 500 percent over the level in 1960. Much has been made of the evils of the federal deficit, but, for purposes of comparison, the gross debt of the federal government rose at a much slower rate during the same period; it increased by 169 percent. Full-faith-and-credit bonds outstanding rose by 442 percent between 1960 and 1978 while nonguaranteed debt rose by 564 percent; except for 1973, the amount of nonguaranteed debt outstanding was at least as large as the amount of voter-approved debt.

The statistics on local government debt outstanding shown in Table 9 reveal a similar pattern. Total debt outstanding rose rapidly between 1960 and 1978, but the increase was not as dramatic as for state gov-

Table 9

LONG-TERM LOCAL GOVERNMENT DEBT BY TYPE
SELECTED YEARS, 1960–1978
(millions of dollars)

Year	Total	Full Faith and Credit	Nonguaranteed	Nonguaranteed as Percent of Total
1960	48,673	32,738	15,938	32.7
1962	55,931	38,008	17,923	32.0
1964	63,126	42,119	21,007	33.3
1965	67,969	44,598	23,371	34.4
1966	72,497	47,091	25,405	35.0
1967	75,962	48,292	27,220	36.1
1968	79,109	50,380	28,730	36.3
1969	86,559	54,694	31,866	36.8
1970	92,512	57,601	34,911	37.7
1971	99,296	62,523	36,773	37.0
1972	108,556	71,009	37,457	34.5
1973	116,905	74,502	42,403	36.3
1974	128,256	80,095	48,161	37.6
1975	133,890	81,836	52,054	38.9
1976	142,941	92,222	50,718	35.5
1977	156,963	94,837	62,126	39.6
1978	182,853	97,099	85,753	46.9

SOURCE: Tax Foundation, *Facts and Figures on Government Finance* (Washington, D.C.: Tax Foundation, Inc., 1979), p. 253.

ernments—a reflection of the more stringent borrowing constraints that the states have placed on municipalities, counties, and townships. Overall, long-term local debt outstanding rose by 276 percent. However, the composition has changed markedly over time. In 1960, there was more than $2 of long-term full-faith-and-credit debt outstanding for each $1 of nonguaranteed debt—nonguaranteed debt was less than one-third of total local government long-term debt. By 1978, however, nonguaranteed debt represented almost one-half of total debt outstanding. While voter-approved indebtedness tripled between 1960 and 1978, the amount of nonguaranteed long-term local bonds outstanding in 1978 was more than five times as large as in 1960. The data show a clear acceleration in the use of nonguaranteed debt. Between 1977 and 1978, nonguaranteed debt outstanding rose by $23.6 billion; this one-year rise was greater than the total increase of the preceding five-year period.

43

The growing addiction of municipal politicians to off-budget borrowing can be more readily seen by considering the volume of sales of *new* long-term municipal securities as shown in Table 10. In 1966, total new borrowing of all local governments was approximately $11 billion, with $1.59 worth of voter-approved bonds issued for each $1 of nonguaranteed bonds. Through 1976, total borrowing rose rapidly to $35.4 billion, but the volume of new full-faith-and-credit debt issued always exceeded the amount of off-budget borrowing, although in 1973 the amounts were nearly equal. From 1975 onward, off-budget borrowing greatly exceeded the amount of voter-approved bond issues. By 1980, $2.50 of new nonguaranteed debt was issued for every $1 of full-faith-and-credit debt, and the total amount financed was almost five times as large as the total in 1966, only 14 years earlier. As the tax revolt of the 1970s intensified and public dissatisfaction and distrust of government deepened, the data show that politicians have increasingly

Table 10
SALES OF LONG-TERM MUNICIPAL SECURITIES
BY TYPE OF SECURITY, 1966–1980
(thousands of dollars)

Year	Full Faith and Credit	Nonguaranteed	Full Faith and Credit Nonguaranteed
1966	$ 6,802,004	$ 4,276,502	1.59
1967	8,944,606	5,460,746	1.64
1968	9,275,329	7,044,178	1.32
1969	7,735,674	3,966,354	1.95
1970	11,851,771	6,230,738	1.90
1971	15,218,492	9,720,572	1.57
1972	13,329,028	10,363,384	1.29
1973	12,269,799	11,651,678	1.04
1974	13,126,341	10,458,468	1.26
1975	15,974,335	24,685,087	1.09
1976	18,200,098	27,215,585	1.06
1977	18,228,339	28,587,547	.63
1978	17,789,591	30,400,140	.59
1979	12,090,955	31,217,952	.39
1980	14,102,312	34,265,490	.41

SOURCE: *Statistical Yearbook of Municipal Finance* (New York: Public Securities Association, 1981), p. 124.

responded not by reducing the size and scope of the public sector but rather by disguising its activities through off-budget devices.

From the perspective of the taxpayer, there should be as much concern about nonguaranteed debt as with full-faith-and-credit debt because in both cases the taxpayer is ultimately liable for repayment. In theory, taxes are raised to repay principal and to cover interest charges for guaranteed debt. Although the same commitment is not *explicitly* made for nonguaranteed bonds, there is a very strong implied commitment that the debt of off-budget enterprises is backed by the taxing power of the public sector. Since there are no guarantees that revenues will be sufficient to cover operating expenses and debt, in almost all cases where revenues are insufficient government subsidies and grants are provided from taxes to avoid default. The number of OBE bankruptcies is miniscule over the past several decades. Such statistics do not imply that OBEs are profitable and efficiently managed operations, but rather that politicians simply cannot afford to permit the off-budget borrowing bubble to burst. Large numbers of OBE financial failures would cause serious concern in the bond markets and would make the issuance of debt difficult. Elected officials cannot rely on the voter to approve bond referenda, so that off-budget borrowing is essential. The off-budget antics at the state and local levels of government are reviewed in detail in Chapters IV and V.

Although it would be useful to have statistics on OBE employment, they are not available and would be all but impossible to collect. It is sufficient to note, however, that the employees of OBEs are not counted in the official statistics issued by state and local governments. Given the total number of off-budget operations, it is reasonable to assume that thousands of individuals who are not counted as public sector employees actually work for public corporations. All statistics on public sector employment, therefore, understate the true size of government.

The ABCs of OBEs

Every action of government produces winners—those who obtain net benefits—and losers—those who pay more in costs than they receive in benefits. The establishment of an OBE is no exception to this general rule. In each case, the winners from public policy actions have strong incentives to form interest groups to lobby elected officials so that each OBE generates a powerful political constituency whose interest may (and frequently does) conflict with the interests of the taxpayers. To illustrate this concept, it is helpful to trace briefly the chain of events in off-budget activity. In general terms, the cast of characters in an off-

45

budget scenario can be classified into four groups: the politicians who create the OBE, the directors and managers of the enterprise, those who provide financing (including the bondholders or lenders), and the suppliers and, in some cases, the recipients, of goods and services from the OBE's operations.[5]

The Politician

The primary reasons that politicians favor off-budget activity have already been discussed at some length: Debt limits may restrict government borrowing or recalcitrant voters may have rejected bond referenda at the polls. Even if neither of these two possibilities applied, there are politically attractive reasons to operate off-budget. All politicians are interested in having patronage jobs or plum positions for their supporters and contributors. Civil service regulations and public sector unions make it difficult for a politician elected to office to use the spoils system. OBEs, however, are free from such inconvenient encumbrances, since civil service regulations do not apply to these organizations. Thus, political allies can be appointed to the OBE's board of directors or management and hired as workers in the organization.

A key feature of all OBEs is their freewheeling style of operation—few of the checks and balances that have evolved in general government to protect the taxpayer are employed. For example, competitive bidding on contracts is a standard feature of virtually all general purpose governments, implemented to assure equal access to bidders and the lowest prices to the public sector. In contrast, OBEs are permitted to negotiate with suppliers so that contracts can be awarded on the basis of political considerations rather than economic factors. Basically, the elected official views the OBE and its off-budget operations as a tool for achieving political goals. Whether these objectives are in the best interests of the taxpayer is questionable. Certainly, as shown in Chapters IV and V, there are numerous cases where political interests and the public interest have collided rather than coincided.

The procedure for establishing an OBE is relatively straightforward: A unit of local government or the state government enacts an ordinance or piece of legislation specifying the legal functions of the corporation, a corporate charter is issued, a board of directors appointed, and the OBE is off and running.

[5]For an in-depth discussion and a number of pithy examples of the roles of these various groups, see Annmarie Walsh, *The Public's Business* (Cambridge, Mass.: MIT Press, 1978), esp. pp. 169–229.

Boards and Managers

In contrast to the private corporation where members of the board of directors are, in theory, responsible to and elected by shareholders, board members of state-level OBEs are usually appointed by the governor and, for municipal OBEs, the directors are appointed by the mayor or city council. There are no shareholders with a financial stake in the public corporation who must be satisfied; rather, board appointees are responsible to political interests and the good will of elected officials for reappointment when their terms expire. The notion that board members are concerned solely with service to the public and are immune from political pressure is a myth. Rarely is there a salary paid for service on the OBE board, although directors' fees and expenses are not uncommon. Board members are usually selected from politically active individuals in the business community to provide "business expertise," but only on a part-time basis. The major function of these individuals is to lend their prestige to the undertaking so that it appears to prospective lenders that competence and expertise are at the helm of the organization. Not infrequently, board members may be involved in business activities that are directly related to those of the OBE, such as banking and construction. Although blatant conflicts of interest may prevent outright financial gain on the part of the board members, they may be able to inconspicuously direct the business dealings of the organization in such a way that political supporters of the board member's patron benefit. It is much easier to manipulate contract awards when competitive bidding is not required, as is the case with OBEs; campaign contributions and support in election contests can influence the dealings of a political organization. Having accepted an appointment to an OBE board, a prestigious businessman benefits by having the organization "succeed" in achieving its stated purpose and in furthering his own business and political objectives through the judicious awarding of contracts and the placement of supporters in patronage positions. In no way is the board member directly responsible to the voter or taxpayer and, once appointed to a term in office, is quite secure in that position—politicians rarely remove directors from OBE boards. There is, then, considerable latitude for the board member to pursue his own self-interest whether the taxpayer approves or is served well or not.

Managers of the OBE are responsible for the day-to-day operations of the OBE, which are supposedly carried out under the policies set by the board. There is no doubt that the manager has considerable discre-

47

tion in regard to his actions, for part-time board members have little time or inclination to become intimately involved with the details of the operations. The critical yardstick by which management is judged is the financial viability of the OBE. As long as the OBE can generate revenues which cover its operating costs and debt service, it is financially independent and insulated from the controls of the government entity that created it. An OBE in financial straits may have difficulty in the credit markets and must return to the sponsoring governmental unit to seek grants and subsidies. At that point, the operations of the OBE come under legislative scrutiny, the efficacy of management may be questioned, and questions may arise about management practices—a most undesirable state of affairs. For this reason, there are pressures placed on OBE management to avoid risky undertakings which may be "unprofitable;" there are strong incentives to "cream the market" by engaging only in activities that generate large amounts of revenue relative to the associated costs regardless of the consequences for the public interest. For example, the construction of toll roads and bridges are remunerative undertakings, but massive congestion may result when toll roads feed city streets ill-equipped to handle large volumes of traffic.

The managers of the OBE largely control the agenda presented to the Board for approval and, because of their intimate knowledge of the organization's operations and finances, can influence the board's decisions on policy matters. The managers are the full-time experts, and the board is heavily dependent on them for advice.

The myth that OBEs have all the advantages of private sector efficiency and none of the disadvantages of public sector inefficiency is widely accepted. OBEs, in short, are supposed to be "businesslike." However, the manager of the OBE enjoys benefits that any private sector manager would greatly envy. When established, every OBE is granted, by legislative fiat, a monopoly on the good or service that it produces. Off-budget electric utilities, for example, do not have competitors. There are, of course, monopolies in the private sector, but these without exception are heavily regulated and such matters as rate changes are conducted openly before regulatory commissions who seek, or at least permit, public input. OBEs are exempt from regulatory review and do not bear the costly expense of preparing cases for rate hearings. Because of their quasi-public status, they pay no taxes or license fees and post no performance bonds; they are also exempted from much of the paperwork and regulatory red tape that strangle the private sector. There are also no legal restrictions on collective bargaining arrangements, and many have the power to override local zoning and building ordinances.

Some of the powers available to OBEs can, indeed, be described as awesome and far beyond any given to private or on-budget government enterprises. For example, in Pennsylvania a municipal OBE may be granted the right of eminent domain that extends beyond the boundaries of the municipality that created it and is specifically exempted from antitrust laws regarding price fixing. Although the powers vary from state to state, all OBE managers are able to operate in secrecy and, in many cases, are not even subjected to legislative review on a regular basis. Robert Moses, as head of the Port of New York Authority, refused successfully the demands of Congress for access to the organization's books. Not only does the taxpayer who directly or indirectly supports these off-budget operations have no explicit control over the management of the enterprise, even elected officials as taxpayers' representatives may have only limited influence over many of the organization's decisions.

OBE managers, however, clearly understand that their positions ultimately depend on the good graces of the board members, who in turn are responsive to political pressures. It is in the best interests of managers to accommodate the political motivations by providing patronage positions. There are ample incentives to encourage managers to expand the operations of the OBE to provide additional job opportunities and to increase cash flow to the organization. After operating expenses and debt-service charges have been paid, the excess revenue is held internally (no "profits" are typically paid to the sponsoring unit of government) and may be used by management for perquisites. Thus, there are ample reasons for OBE managers to be "growth oriented" and to expand their empires rapidly, even if it requires a broad interpretation of the organization's mission. Robert Moses, over a period of decades, built the Port of New York Authority into a financial giant and had enormous sums of money at his disposal. Few are aware that this entity has vast real estate interests including the World Trade Center in New York City and control over airports, bridges, toll roads, restaurants, and harbor facilities. Whether the public benefits from the growth orientation of OBE managers is not clear; what is certain, however, is that OBE managers have considerable latitude in their decision-making and, at least to some extent, are influenced by political pressures.

As is true of any economic entity, the financial arrangements are of critical importance to the OBE, for without access to the bond markets as a source of capital, the organization is doomed. Ultimately, the board and managers must satisfy the bondholders who are private individuals as well as institutional investors, e.g., banks and pension funds. The bondholders have claim only to the repayment of the principal and interest on the OBE's debt and no claim whatsoever on any excess revenues generated. Nor do investors have any control over the activities of managers or directors or any voice in their selection. The interests of the bondholders are protected by an indenture agreement, basically a contract between the OBE and bondholders, that is administered by a bank that serves as trustee on behalf of the bondholders. Indenture agreements impose conditions on OBE operations in order to protect the financial interests of bondholders. Accounting procedures may be specified in these documents as can conditions on reserve fund balances, maintenance levels, prices, and even on new projects. Much of the touted flexibility of the OBE can be lost by the specification of very restrictive terms in the indentures. The bank receives income for its services as a trustee and may also be able to sell its services as financial advisor to the entity. Because trustees' income rises as the volume of debt issued by OBEs increases, bankers have incentives to encourage new projects and new issues of debt. Thus, the banking community is a group with a vested interest in the growth of off-budget enterprise.

When bonds are issued, underwriters perform the function of middlemen between the OBE (the borrower) and lenders. Underwriters purchase the bonds in wholesale lots at a discount and sell them to private investors. The income from underwriting results from the spread between the price at which bonds are bought at wholesale and the price obtained from selling the bonds. For government agencies, the spread is determined by competitive bidding among underwriters, but an OBE may place the bonds with a given underwriter or a group of underwriters on a noncompetitive basis which leads to higher spreads. A great deal of money in underwriting can be at stake in the placement of even a single bond issue. The income of underwriters also increases as the volume of debt issued rises so that underwriters also have an economic stake in the expansion of the debt of existing OBEs and in the creation of new ones.

The legal profession is also actively engaged in the financial machinations of OBEs in the form of "bond counsels." These attorneys receive payment for reviewing the specifications of the indenture and issuing an opinion on whether the bond issue conforms to the requirements which makes it exempt from federal taxation. Here again, the amount of payment received for legal service is dependent upon the volume of debt issued; income rises with OBE borrowing.

Suppliers of Services

OBE debt is issued to obtain capital to build some facility such as a power plant, an airport, a water supply system, or a highway. Because most, if not all, OBEs are operating organizations lacking their own construction capability, a capital construction project implies that work will be awarded to consultants, architects, engineers, excavators, building contractors, and a whole range of specialists in such fields to bring the project to completion. In addition, these consultants and contractors employ workers and use the products and services of numerous suppliers. All of these individuals have a vested interest in the expansion of off-budget activities for it implies profits for employers and work for employees. As is the case in the financial aspects of OBEs, competitive bidding is not required on contracts to those who provide goods and services. The lowest price on a bid (if there is one) is no guarantee that a contract will be awarded to a given firm. In such cases, the contract can be awarded by the OBE managers on the basis of "back scratching." The contractor who assists the OBE manager the most in achieving this goal will be favored over others. At least in part, the contract awards are based on political considerations, for those involved in the financial aspects of the OBE and in supply services can help the OBE manager obtain political favors in the form of grants and subsidies from the legislature, and they form a powerful interest group. Labor unions representing construction workers, for example, are politically active and very well financed.

In addition, the recipients of services from off-budget enterprises can bring political pressure to bear. Many localities have off-budget housing authorities to build subsidized, low-income housing. Those individuals who are eligible for low-income housing assistance have a strong incentive to encourage the construction of additional units and have organizations which lobby for this, and other, favors.

As the discussion above demonstrates, each off-budget entity does not exist in isolation, but cooperates with other groups to carry out its mission. Internally, there are pressures for the expansion of the OBE and, externally, every OBE has interest groups which also benefit from ever-expanding OBE activity. The benefits are concentrated among interest groups which have strong incentives to support the OBE in its search for tax subsidies and grants. The costs of expansion are dispersed widely across all taxpayers who have little real financial incentive to organize in order to oppose OBE growth. The off-budget enterprise is an organization created by politicians for political purposes and the entity is permeated with political considerations. Whether the social benefits provided by off-budget devices exceed the associated costs is questionable, and a number of issues must be considered before an appropriate answer can be found.

The Rhetoric and Reality of Off-Budget Enterprise

No prudent politican is likely to admit publicly that the primary justification for off-budget enterprises is that his political goals may be more effectively attained if constitutional or statutory limits on debt can be evaded. Rather, it is essential to the politican that the public perceive the operations of OBEs to be in the public interest, rather than merely acts of fiscal legerdemain. If it is assumed that the activities undertaken by OBEs are, in fact, legitimately carried out by the public rather than by the private sector, why then should these activities be undertaken off-budget rather than on-budget? Inevitably the politician's answer to this question is that OBEs are more flexible and innovative than bureaucratic government. There are costs associated with off-budget operations, however, that are higher than would be the case if activities were undertaken on-budget. Both general obligation bonds and OBE bonds are traded in the municipal market and, although both are tax exempt, the interest rate on OBE obligations is always higher than for full-faith-and-credit borrowing. The reason for the higher borrowing costs for OBE obligations is that this debt is perceived in the markets to carry somewhat higher risk. Moreover, some of the services required for the placement of OBE debt, such as bond counsel provided by attorneys and trustee fees, would be avoided or lower if debt were issued by units of government rather than by their corporate offspring. The point is that the alleged flexibility and innovation of OBEs is not achieved at zero cost; there are very real financial costs incurred when off-budget rather than on-budget debt is issued. In addition, a large volume of economic research in the field of public choice over the past several years have shown that it is above-board political competition, not bureaucratic isolation, which provides incentives, however weak, for cost effectiveness in the public sector.[6] The threat of a "takeover bid" by a competing political entrepreneur is virtually nonexistent to the all but tenured OBE manager, but earns the constant attention of state and local politicians. Thus, elementary public choice theory would predict that OBEs would be less cost-conscious than on-budget agencies and that flexibility and independence of government agencies are vices, not virtues from the taxpayer's perspective.[7]

There is little doubt that OBEs can be more flexible in their methods of operation than government agencies; after all, as mentioned earlier, OBEs are exempt from many onerous regulations and restrictions and may be given special powers. Certainly, no case is to be made that units of government are paragons of efficiency. If OBEs are exempted from regulations intended to protect the interests of the public, what assurances are there that the public interest is being served? Apparently, what is good for the goose is not necessarily good for the gander. Either the operating style of the OBE is far superior to that of the public agency or it is not. If it is so superior, why not adopt the same modus operandi for government bureaus? Certainly, basing arguments for off-budget activity on the poorer performance of on-budget units of government is tantamount to damning the public sector with very faint praise.

Another indication that at least some of the widely heralded flexibility of OBEs is undoubtedly a myth is that while the politicians may permit a freewheeling operating style, lenders are not as generous in their attitudes. The bond indentures administered by banks as trustees often contain very detailed and restrictive provisions regarding OBE operations and finance. Thus, some flexibility may be lost or at least severely limited. With regard to the claim that OBEs are inherently "innovative," there are many questions about whether the innovations developed by some OBEs have been good or bad. Evidence from the case studies

[6]This statement should not be interpreted as an endorsement of the civil service system. In fact, it may be argued that the civil service system has contributed materially to the growth of government, for public employees have job security or tenure and, consequently, take a long-term view of the economic gains to be achieved by expanding the size and scope of their agencies. Under the spoils system, turnover would be virtually assured at least every eight years and there would be much less incentive for the individual employee to build an "empire" within the bureaucracy, given that it would evaporate with a change in administrations.

[7]See, for example, George Stigler, "Economic Competition and Political Competition," *Public Choice*, Fall 1973, pp. 91–106. For a review of some of the more recent literature, see Thomas J. DiLorenzo, "The Expenditure Effects of Restricting Competition in Local Public Service Industries: The Case of Special Districts," *Public Choice*, Winter 1981, pp. 569–78.

presented in the chapters that follow indicate clearly that such innovations as "fast track" construction methods have, at least in some instances, been disastrous.

Economists may claim that there is a unique feature of OBEs that makes them desirable: Each OBE ideally must generate its own revenue from services that it provides and, therefore, is subject to some market constraints. An OBE cannot draw from general revenues collected by taxation, but must provide services of some sort for its revenues; in a sense, the organization must meet a form of market test. There is cold comfort in this argument, and the argument is intrinsically flawed, for it still does not provide a rationale for off-budget finance. A unit of on-budget government could be established to perform the same operation and be self-supporting from its own revenue. Besides, as pointed out in detail in Chapters IV and V, many OBEs are far from self-supporting and dip regularly into the tax till. Yet a more fundamental question arises: Are many of the activities undertaken by OBEs appropriate for the public sector or should these be accomplished by the private sector?

A vast amount of economic research has been conducted that compares the cost of a wide range of activities carried on by private firms and by units of local, state, and federal government.[8] In every case, the private sector has been found to be far more efficient than the public sector in that private production results in substantially lower unit costs. The evidence is so one-sided and overwhelming that the "Bureaucratic Rule of Two" has been proposed, which holds that the transfer of a service from the private sector to the public sector doubles its unit costs of production. Private companies perform a host of activities that are also conducted by OBEs: electric power generation, trash collection, the construction and operation of hospitals, parking lots, water supply systems, schools, industrial and commercial development projects, housing facilities, and airports, among others. Is it in the public interest to have on-budget or off-budget enterprises produce goods and services when the same quality of output can be produced at much lower cost by market-oriented private firms? In addition, private firms pay taxes and license fees and provide other forms of revenue to the public sector that the less-efficient public firms do not provide. If the public sector refrained from competition with the private sector, then taxes on individuals could be lowered.

Every off-budget enterprise is essentially bureaucratic in character

[8]See James T. Bennett and Manuel H. Johnson, *Better Government at Half the Price* (Ottawa, Ill.: Caroline House Publishers, 1981).

because it is insulated by the monopoly granted by government from the competitive pressures of the marketplace. For the OBE manager, there is no threat that a more efficient competitor may drive his operation out of business. The manager has no real incentives to minimize the costs of production of the services produced by the OBE, for his salary is not determined by the economic performance of the entity, but by the politically motivated board. Excess revenues (income after costs of operation and debt service), if any, are not turned over to the governmental unit sponsoring the entity, but are held internally and may be used to purchase perquisites for the members of the board and the managers. Unlike politicians, board members and managers do not face periodic assessments of their performance in either the political arena or the marketplace and, consequently, have considerable security in their positions. Such conditions are conducive to what economists refer to as "shirking," a relaxed style of management that does not give high priority to cost consciousness. Moreover, whenever decisions are insulated from market pressures and dominated by special interest groups and political considerations, political objectives are inevitably given far more weight than the "public interest."

Whither the Public Interest

The OBE is an oddity: a corporation without stockholders, a creature of the public sector unfettered by many constraints that apply to the public sector, an unregulated monopoly, an "independent" firm which is permeated with political overtones, a nonprofit organization that in many cases displaces profit-seeking (and taxpaying) private firms, and, above all, a quasi-public enterprise supposedly imbued with a sense of the public interest. Undoubtedly, off-budget activities were undertaken because certain goals could be better achieved through back-door finance and spending than through the normal agencies of government. The issue is whether the interests of the taxpayers or the interests of the politicians are enhanced more by the operations of OBEs. The statutory and constitutional restraints on government that OBEs are able to bypass were instituted originally to protect the taxpayer from the profligate proclivities of politicians to borrow and spend excessively. There is ample evidence that such constraints are needed; calls for a constitutional amendment requiring a balanced budget are based on a widely accepted view that neither the Congress nor the administration in power can put the nation's fiscal affairs in order without a constitutional directive. Thus, restraints on public sector fiscal activities have long have been viewed as in the public interest. Is it then reasonable to argue that strategies intended to *evade* these restraints can simultaneously be in the public interest? Although politicians may claim to act in the public interest, the voters are likely to have a better understanding of what they want than their elected officials whose goals and objectives may be different. As documented in the chapters that follow, off-budget devices have frequently been used to finance schemes that voters have repeatedly rejected at the ballot box. To then claim that such actions are in the public interest stretches the imagination beyond tolerable limits. When public operations are conducted on-budget, there is at least some measure of accountability of public servants to the taxpayer. None of this discussion should be interpreted to imply that all on-budget actions of government are, by definition, in the best interests of society at large. It is true, however, that on-budget activity is conducted more openly, and public sector behavior may be challenged periodically in elections.

In the end, the OBE is a creation of the politician who has found that there are inherent advantages to off-budget activity which serve his self-interest: Spending and borrowing can continue without irritating constraint; prudence can be preached while profligacy is pursued; and patronage can be dispensed without civil service restrictions.

H. L. Mencken's view of the politician, cited below, may be overstated, but it raises serious doubts whether the politician's desire for going off-budget is, in fact, to enhance the public interest.

> For if experience teaches us anything at all it teaches us this: that a good politician, under democracy, is quite as unthinkable as an honest burglar. His very existence, indeed, is a standing subversion of the public good in every rational sense. He is not one who serves the common wealth; he is simply one who preys upon the commonwealth. It is to the interest of all the rest of us to hold down his powers to an irreducible minimum, and to reduce his compensation to nothing; it is to his interest to augment his powers at all hazards, and to make his compensation all the traffic will bear. To argue that these aims are identical is to argue palpable nonsense. The politician, at his ideal best, never even remotely approximated in practice, is a necessary evil; at his worst he is an almost intolerable nuisance.[9]

The issues discussed above are difficult, if not impossible, to resolve in abstract terms. Even the notion of what is and what is not in the public interest can change over time, and different individuals may have vastly different opinions about what is best for society. A more

[9]H. L. Mencken, *Prejudices* (New York: Vintage Books, 1955), p. 172.

detailed look at how off-budget activity has been used—and abused—at the local, state, and federal levels of government should provide additional insights into such issues.

IV. Empire Building in the Empire State: The Political Legacy of Nelson Rockefeller

The Constitution, Borrowing, and Spending in New York State

At the state level of government New York is by far the most active in terms of off-budget spending and borrowing, largely because of the late Governor Nelson Rockefeller's efforts, from 1959 to 1974, to create dozens of statewide OBEs, which circumvent constitutional constraints on spending and borrowing. So extensive are off-budget operations in New York State that during the early 1970s, the state accounted for over one-third of all nonguaranteed borrowing in the entire nation. By 1980, the state's off-budget spending was approximately $8 billion, compared to $15 billion in on-budget spending. Also, in that year the debt outstanding of statewide OBEs stood at $23 billion—fully five times larger than the amount of voter-approved general obligation debt.

The evolution of off-budget enterprise in New York State has led to a government which is truly out of control (of the voters). The exuberance of Nelson Rockefeller is largely responsible for the extraordinary subversion of constitutional spending constraints in New York State, and Rockefeller should be regarded as something of a political aberration. Nevertheless, Rockefeller's instincts for political survival—the desire to spend huge sums of money on politically powerful constituent groups while deferring the costs by borrowing—are characteristic of all politicians at all levels of government and, as will be shown, have led to similar results nationwide. The remaining 49 states have created hundreds of OBEs which account for over half of all state government borrowing. These are estimated to spend over $100 billion annually and are routinely used to evade constitutional and statutory constraints on spending and borrowing.

New York State has a referendum requirement for the issuance of state government debt which dates back to 1846. Under the original state constitution of 1777, the legislature was authorized to approve the creation of debt by a majority vote. Using this power, it approved borrowings in the early 1800s for turnpikes, canals, and railroads, as did many other state legislatures. By 1837, New York and several other states were seriously overextended in their borrowing, and during the subsequent financial panic (of 1837), 13 states defaulted on their debt and New York, being on the brink of default, enacted heavy new taxes to meet its borrowing obligations. An indignant taxpaying public demanded that a referendum requirement on future state borrowing be enacted to constrain future political profligacy. Consequently, a referendum requirement to control public borrowing was incorporated into the state constitution in 1846.

The referendum requirement made debt finance more explicit and remained binding until 1921, the year in which the first OBE, the Port Authority of New York and New Jersey, was introduced. By 1938 numerous statewide OBEs had been established providing services ranging from bridges to planetariums.

The proliferation of OBEs was a major concern to participants in the 1938 state constitutional convention, as is illustrated by the following statement in a report by the New York State Constitutional Convention Committee:

> Public authorities bring sharply to the fore the question of popular responsibility. . . . All these authorities perform governmental functions, and have tremendous financial powers, but they are responsive to the control of voters only in that the members of the authority are appointed by a popularly elected executive. . . . But once an authority is established, it is almost self-perpetuating. Sometimes the activities of an authority transcend in financial scope the activities of a whole town or village, but they have none of the elements of popular control which accrue as a matter of course to the town or village.[1]

These concerns over the establishment of OBEs were largely ignored for the next 20 years as 13 additional OBEs were formed. What seemed at the time the seeds of a financial and political problem to the taxpayers of New York State sprouted into totally unrestrained spending and borrowing by the early 1960s, under the direction of Governor Rockefeller, who, by 1975, had led the state to default and bankruptcy. A review of the causes and consequences of the proliferation of OBEs in New York State during the past 20 years provides useful insights into the political economy of constitutional spending and borrowing limitation.

[1]New York State, *Report of the New York State Constitutional Convention Committee,* Vol. IV (Albany, N.Y.: 1928), p. 191.

Nelson Rockefeller: Off-Budget Operations and Fiscal Responsibility

When Nelson Rockefeller first occupied the governor's mansion in Albany in 1959, it was with one overriding objective: to become President of the United States. When asked by a reporter when he first thought of being president, he responded, "Ever since I was a kid. After all, when you think of what I had, what else was there to aspire to?"[2] Upon taking office in 1959, Rockefeller immediately used Albany as his base of operations to try to secure the 1960 Republican presidential nomination. His mammoth campaign organization led presidential historian Theodore White to allude to John F. Kennedy's organization as a "Montana road show" by comparison.[3] Rockefeller's intention was clearly, and quite rationally (from a politician's standpoint), to build up a huge constituency, as quickly as possible, at the taxpayers' expense. His years in the governor's mansion were a time of investing in human capital—in demonstrating that he was indeed capable of managing a large enterprise, i.e., one similar to that worthy of a president's attention. The governor came into office with a master plan to greatly expand the state's programs in the areas of education, health care, welfare, housing, and many others. The initial expansion of these programs, which was both rapid and extensive, was financed largely through borrowing and tax increases. During Rockefeller's first five years in office there were numerous tax increases: In 1959 the cigarette tax was increased from three cents to five cents per pack; the estate tax rose; gasoline taxes were increased from four cents to six cents per gallon; personal income tax withholding was instituted and three new rate brackets were created; and a 15 percent tobacco-products tax was established. These tax increases constituted the largest ever enacted by the New York State legislature at the time. After this first-year raid on the taxpayers' pocketbooks, insurance taxes were created in 1961 and were accelerated in 1962, and alcoholic beverage control license fees were increased by 25 to 50 percent, along with many other miscellaneous charges.[4] Total tax receipts rose at an annual rate of 12.6 percent during Rockefeller's first four years in office, compared to an annual growth

[2]As quoted in P. D. McClelland and A. L. Magdovitz, *Crisis in the Making: The Political Economy of New York State Since 1945* (Cambridge: Cambridge University Press, 1981), p. 172.

[3]Ibid., p. 173.

[4]Ibid., p. 94.

rate of 7.5 percent during the preceding four years,[5] and generated much taxpayer discontent.

Taxpayer opposition to Rockefeller's spending plans was repeatedly ignored by the governor throughout his tenure by simply financing various projects through off-budget enterprises. For example, when voters rejected a $100 million housing bond issue for the third time, Governor Rockefeller created the Housing Finance Authority, which issued massive amounts of nonguaranteed debt, at one point in excess of the entire guaranteed debt of New York State. In 1961, voters rejected a $500 million higher-education bond issue for the fourth time; the Governor created the off-budget State University Construction Fund. In 1965, the voters rejected, for the fifth time, a housing bond issue; the Governor created the Urban Development Corporation. In 1962, Rockefeller's fourth year as governor, there were 125 OBEs in New York State, 26 of them statewide, with a total outstanding debt of $3.3 billion. By the time he resigned from office in 1973, 14 months before the state faced default and bankruptcy, OBE debt had quadrupled. At $13.3 billion, the debt was approximately four times the amount of guaranteed, voter-approved borrowing, and the debt of the Housing Finance Authority alone exceeded the entire guaranteed debt of the state by about 50 percent![6] The constitutionally imposed referendum requirement for the issuance of state debt obviously placed no effective constraint whatever on the ambitious (to say the least) spending plans of Rockefeller and other state politicians for, as one author has put it, when it came to public expenditure, Rockefeller "approached the world with all the deference of a runaway locomotive."[7] One of the first "stops" along the way, once Rockefeller was on board in the governor's mansion, was the subsidization of middle-income housing.

Underground Housing in New York State

New York City's housing problems have been well-publicized and were perhaps epitomized by the scene set when candidate Ronald Reagan visited the South Bronx in the summer of 1980, surrounded by what appeared to be Berlin in the spring of 1945. One of the root causes of New York City's housing shortage and deterioration problem is rent control, which has been in effect there since 1943. After the Second World War, federal rent controls were lifted, but were retained in New

[5]New York State, *Annual Report of the Comptroller*, various volumes.
[6]Ibid.
[7]McClelland and Magdovitz, p. 170.

York City. The predictable effects soon became all too apparent: The controls artificially stimulated housing demand, while reducing supply, given that the price of rental housing was set below the market price. The resultant shortages have been accompanied by severe deterioration of the housing stock as well, as is apparent in the South Bronx, for landlords have little incentive to invest in building repair if at least part of the cost cannot be passed on in the form of higher rents. The effects of 40 years of rent control have been aptly described by columnist Robert Bleiberg:

> Vast stretches of real estate in at least three of five boroughs have decayed beyond the point of no return. Ancient tenements and (until recently) quite habitable buildings alike stand empty, boarded up and stripped, vandalized and blackened by fire. Some no longer stand at all except in piles of broken brick and rubble. Whole blocks of Brooklyn and the Bronx have been compared by expert witnesses to the bombed-out ruins of London and Berlin.[8]

There are two general policy approaches to these problems. First, abandoning rent control would provide incentives for housing construction and maintenance, which would eventually eliminate the shortages. Second, rent controls can be maintained and the taxpayers can subsidize the middle and upper-income individuals who comprise the large majority of those who are made worse off because of the rent controls. Needless to say, the latter alternative is the most popular among politicians, for it is always more beneficial politically to dispense subsidies to politically influential groups, the costs of which are widely dispersed among all taxpayers, than to allow market forces to work. New York State initiated a system of housing subsidies in 1955, but throughout the late 1950s voter support for New York City housing subsidies waned. Some bond referenda were passed, but upstate voters consistently opposed them and by 1959 Rockefeller acknowledged that the housing subsidy program was "virtually at a stand-still."[9] That, of course, was the way the voters wanted it. The Governor immediately established a task force to "study" the state's housing problems. After some deliberation, the task force concluded that two problems had to be addressed: using state subsidies to "alleviate the housing shortages," and placing such housing "within the means of middle-income families." The task force's final report concluded that the state should

[8]Robert M. Bleiberg, "Rotten Boroughs: New York City Has Been Undermined by Rent Control," *Barron's*, October 27, 1975, p. 7.
[9]McClelland and Magdovitz, p. 201.

develop an off-budget housing finance agency, since the voters disapproved of on-budget financing proposals. Rockefeller complied by creating the Housing Finance Authority (HFA) in 1960, which within 15 years had exceeded its original debt ceiling by a factor of 10.

Establishing the HFA enabled Rockefeller to ignore both the voters and the state's constitution, but he still faced problems getting investors to lend the vast sums he had in mind, given the uncertainty over future revenues from the proposed projects. To deal with this problem, Rockefeller called upon John Mitchell, a well-known municipal bond lawyer (later, of Watergate fame in his role as attorney general of the United States during the Nixon administration). Mitchell believed that the HFA would have difficulty marketing revenue bonds because the revenues from rental housing were more uncertain than, for example, tolls on bridges and highways. The investment community would therefore charge higher interest rates, forcing the agency to increase rents, and reducing the demand for the agency's "product." Mitchell solved this dilemma by inventing the "moral obligation bond." This constitutional end-run requires the issuing agency to create a debt-service reserve fund out of the proceeds of its bonds. If at any time the agency cannot pay the debt service on the bonds *and* should a shortfall occur in that fund, then it is "incumbent upon the Legislature to consider the apportionment and payment of the amounts of money to restore that capital reserve fund."[10] Now, by New York law, no legislature of the present can bind a future legislature into appropriating funds. Therefore, the above phrase is not legally but, as Mitchell reasoned, is "morally" binding. Future legislatures may decide to honor a commitment to cover a shortfall, but then again they may not. Thus, since the legislature is not legally obliged to appropriate money, the referendum requirement does not apply. More importantly, investors took the "moral obligation" seriously—they were convinced that the Governor would see to it that the HFA would not default, which would, of course, draw much public attention to these shenanigans—the type of attention the Governor wanted to avoid. In addition, the Comptroller of the Currency declared that HFA's bonds were (in reality, if not legally) "general obligations" of the state. The HFA therefore started out selling its bonds at an interest charge nearly identical to that paid by the state on its general obligation debt.

[10]New York State Moreland Act Commission, *Restoring Credit and Confidence: A Reform Program for New York State and its Public Authorities* (Albany: State Printing Office, 1976), p. 109.

Having placed the appropriate off-budget mechanisms in place, Rockefeller departed upon one of his famed spending binges. The debt outstanding of the HFA soon outstripped that of the state itself, and the HFA became the largest issuer of moral obligation debt in the nation. Although the subsidization of middle-income housing was the original purpose for creating the HFA, it was used as a mechanism to evade voter rejection of various proposals totally unrelated to housing. This was done by incorporating into the HFA separate funds—financed by issuing moral obligation bonds—for state university construction (after a higher education bond issue was rejected for the fourth time in 1961), mental health facilities, nursing homes, voluntary hospitals, municipal hospitals, municipal mental facilities, senior citizen centers, and many other services. Voter-approved borrowing for these services is only a small fraction of the total commitments. In health and higher education, for example, voter-approved debt stood at $283 million by 1975, whereas the moral obligation debt of the HFA approached $6 billion—approximately 21 times the amount of voter-approved debt.[11]

Life in the Fast Lane: "Fast Track" Construction Methods and the Urban Development Corporation

Having gained the support (and affection?) of many middle-income earners through the activities of the HFA, Rockefeller turned his attention to low-income housing in the mid-1960s. The voters of the state, however, were of a different mind. Between 1961 and 1965 five propositions for low-income housing construction were presented to the voters and were overwhelmingly defeated. Facing public disapproval of the bond issues, Rockefeller proposed a type of super off-budget agency that would serve to subsidize both low-income housing and industrial development. The Urban Development Corporation (UDC) was to have powers of eminent domain, the power to receive grants, the power to override local zoning and building code controls, and "the freedom from various 'restrictions' which would prevent rapid development."[12] The elected representatives of the State General Assembly, following the cue given them by the voters, voted down the proposed UDC on the morning of April 9, 1968, by a vote of 86 to 45. Infuriated, Rockefeller and his staff spent the entire day threatening punishment if the legislators did not cooperate with the Governor, and by 11:30 that evening the Assembly reversed its vote and approved the

[11]Ibid., p. 92
[12]Ibid., p. 118.

creation of the UDC by a vote of 86 to 45! The next day, the Governor signed a bill which sharply increased the legislators' pensions. When asked about his strong-arm tactics in getting the UDC legislation passed, Rockefeller audaciously responded: "One has to use whatever authority one has when something of major importance to the people comes before you."[13]

As mentioned earlier, speed was of the essence with regard to the UDC's spending programs. By June 1969, 50 projects were underway in 23 cities with estimated construction costs of about $2 billion. This is quite a sum when one considers that *total* state expenditures in that year were approximately $5.5 billion. The emphasis on speed (and recklessness?) was described by the corporation's first director, Edward J. Logue:

> UDC had many ardent supporters who embraced the idea of a broad gauged development agency . . . with a directive to go out and build, build, build.[14]

The UDC's construction methods came to be known as "fast-tracking," which entailed simultaneous work on several aspects of a project, commencement of construction before final project drawings and specifications were completed, and the start-up of construction before all the relevant construction contracts had been signed. Fast-tracking enabled the UDC to spend approximately $8.2 billion on its construction programs from 1969 to 1974 even though its debt authorization, which was apparently ignored, stood at $2 billion in 1972.[15] By contrast, voter-approved capital construction expenditures for the entire state of New York during this period was about $2.9 billion—a mere 35 percent of UDC's expenditures.[16] The rationale for the fast-track method given by the Governor and the staff was that they were concerned about how to save the citizens of the state money during periods of inflation.

Fast-Tracking Into Bankruptcy

Because of its insulation from taxpayer preferences, the UDC (as well as other OBEs) soon became grossly inefficient, even by the standards of other government-run enterprises. By February 25, 1975, with over $1 billion in partially completed construction, over $1 billion in outstanding bonds, and operating costs of about $1 million per day, the

[13]As cited in McClelland and Magdovitz, p. 103.
[14]New York State Moreland Act Commission, p. 125.
[15]Ibid., p. 127.
[16]Ibid.

financial markets closed to the UDC. UDC had no funds with which to pay its outstanding obligations, and the banks were unwilling to award it any new financing. Financial planning had been little or no concern to either the Governor or UDC Director Logue. In testimony before the Moreland Act Commission on the UDC, Logue described his rationale for ignoring all financial constraints:

> I communicated to the Governor's office that we wanted to increase our bond authorization from one billion to two billion dollars. This was in late 1971 or at the latest early '72. . . . I don't think I would have taken the job in the first place and left Boston if all I was going to do is be involved in a billion dollar operation. I have spent that much or more or got others to spend that much in one city, in Boston, in six years.[17]

When told by UDC's treasurer that borrowing of the magnitude Logue had in mind would not be feasible, he responded:

> I do not believe there is any evidence to support your conclusion . . . we are going to build as much as we can. The need is here now. When . . . we have gone as far as we can go, and we can't borrow anymore, that is another day. Please table that concern. I don't consider it relevant at this time.[18]

As anyone who works for a living knows, this statement is a sure-fire recipe for bankruptcy. With such reckless financial planning the state soon began to subsidize the operations of the UDC despite all the claims of "self-sufficiency" prior to its establishment. Between mid-1968 and early 1971, UDC received approximately $63 million in state subsidies which have increased at an accelerating rate to this day.[19]

With this attitude toward financial planning, which was heartily endorsed and encouraged by the Governor, the UDC's "fast-tracking" construction methods generated the extraordinary risks that eventually led to its being shut off from the financial markets. The types of risks assumed as part of UDC's fast-tracking methods are as follows:[20]

1. UDC would proceed into construction with excavation and foundation work while final plan and engineering studies for the project's superstructure were unfinished. If unfavorable subsoil conditions were

---

[17]Ibid., p. 129.

[18]Ibid., p. 137.

[19]Ibid., p. 130. In 1961 Rockefeller had the state accounting laws altered to delete these subsidies from the budget document.

[20]Ibid., p. 224.

uncovered or if design changes were later required, the required modifications could eliminate any savings due to time saving.

2. UDC's building contracts were most often negotiated with a single builder rather than competitively bid, which raised contract prices.

3. UDC proceeded with projects without signing final construction contracts or agreements to deliver performance bonds. For example, as of June 30, 1974, three projects costing about $4.9 million were underway without any formal contracts.

4. Construction would typically begin before UDC was actually given title to the land upon which construction was taking place. By June 30, 1971, 14 such projects were underway, and had already incurred $16,026,000 in construction costs out of a proposed total of $242,850,000. UDC's proclaimed strategy here was to reduce the legislature's incentives to terminate projects by accumulating nonrecoverable costs.

5. UDC would commence construction prior to receiving building commitments for federal HUD subsidies. This practice led to severe financial trouble in January 1973 when President Nixon announced a moratorium on further subsidy payments under Section 236 of the National Housing Act.

The UDC defaulted on February 25, 1975, approximately 14 months after Nelson Rockefeller resigned as governor to head for bigger and better things in Washington. UDC's default imperiled the credit worthiness of the entire state and every agency of the state subsequently paid higher rates for its borrowed funds. Ironically, the "solution" to the default problem which the state legislature and Governor Hugh Carey developed was to create yet another OBE, the Project Finance Agency, which could start afresh using the moral obligation bond device to pay the bills of the bankrupt UDC and to subsidize the operations of various other OBEs. The natural solution to the problem of bankruptcy caused by excessive borrowing was therefore even more borrowing, given the politician's aversion to cutting spending as a way of dealing with fiscal crises. The borrowing bubble has not yet burst, but the state's financial position is anything but healthy. Furthermore, the rescue mission undertaken by the legislature in no way limits the future use of moral obligation debt by the state's OBEs.

The Rest of the Iceberg

The HFA and the UDC are just the tip of the off-budget iceberg in New York State, although it is true that the financial problems created by these agencies are of titanic proportions. Off-budget enterprises have been used to evade constitutional borrowing limitations ever since the Port Authority of New York was created in 1921, and have increased in both number and size ever since. Table 11 lists selected *statewide* OBEs created from 1921 to 1975. There are now over 40 statewide OBEs, and over 230, including local OBEs, throughout the entire state. The responses of the HFA and UDC to voter rejection of proposed government spending plans during the late 1950s to the early 1970s are typical of the general response of all the state's OBEs to the fiscal restraint desired by voters. Figure 1 plots the amounts of general obligation debt of the State of New York and the nonguaranteed OBE debt from 1960 to 1975. As seen there, when Rockefeller took office, total OBE debt was slightly over $3 billion, three times larger than the state's general obligation debt. By 1976 total OBE debt outstanding was approximately $18.9 billion, over five times the $3.6 billion general obligation debt of the state.

This plethora of OBEs constitutes a constant drain on the taxpayer's pocketbook for several reasons. Each OBE is granted a monopoly status by government fiat, and can therefore charge a monopoly price far in excess of actual costs. For example, the Port Authority of New York and New Jersey, which has a monopoly on Hudson River crossings and air travel facilities in the New York City area, takes in *net* receipts in excess of $100 million per year.[21] The major beneficiaries of these monopoly profits are the managers of the Port Authority, who are better able to continue along their empire-building ways to finance bureaucratic perquisites, such as the billion-dollar World Trade Center which houses hundreds of government offices.

Real estate development projects such as the World Trade Center are sure to be undertaken more efficiently by private sector firms, given the inherent inefficiences of public enterprises such as the Port Authority, but are precluded from doing so. The Port Authority avoids risky projects such as mass transit facilities like the plague, for such projects would threaten its ability to accumulate budget surpluses.

Many of the other OBEs are not so fortunate as to have access to the easy pluckings of toll bridges, bus terminals, and rail facilities. Deficits are actually the rule more than the exception among the state's OBEs, and state subsidies place an even greater drain on the taxpayer's income. State appropriations in support of OBEs amounted to over $2 billion, or approximately $115 per capita, in 1980, as shown in Table 12. The data in Table 12 provide an estimate of the total amount of financial

---

[21]New York State, Office of the Comptroller, *Statewide Public Authorities: Individual Authority Summaries* (Albany, N.Y.: Office of the Comptroller, 1972).

Table 11
STATEWIDE OBEs IN NEW YORK

Agency	Year Created
Port Authority of New York and New Jersey	1921
Albany Port District Commission	1925
Lake Champlain Bridge Commission	1927
Niagara Frontier Bridge Commission	1929
Whiteface Mountain Bridge Commission	1929
Power Authority of the State of New York	1931
New York State Bridge Authority	1932
American Museum of National History Planetarium Authority	1933
Bethpage Park Authority	1933
Buffalo and Fort Erie Public Bridge Authority	1933
Central New York Regional Market Authority	1933
Industrial Exhibit Authority	1933
Jones Beach State Parkway Authority	1933
Lower Hudson Regional Market Authority	1933
Pelham-Portchester Parkway Authority	1933
Saratoga Spring Authority	1933
Thousand Islands Bridge Authority	1933
Triborough Bridge Authority	1933
Henry Hudson Parkway Authority	1933
Marine Parkway Authority	1934
New York State World War Memorial Authority	1934
Albany Light, Heat, and Power Authority	1935
Albany Regional Market Authority	1935
Queens-Midtown Tunnel Authority	1935
Rockland, Westchester Hudson River Crossing Authority	1935
New York City Tunnel Authority	1936
New York City Parkway Authority	1938
Niagara Frontier Authority	1943
Dormitory Authority	1944
Whiteface Mountain Authority	1944
Triborough Bridge and Tunnel Authority	1946
New York State Thruway Authority	1950
Ogdensburg Bridge Authority	1950

Table 11 cont.
STATEWIDE OBEs IN NEW YORK

Agency	Year Created
Genesee Valley Regional Market Authority	1951
New York City Transit Authority	1953
Niagara Frontier Port Authority	1955
Oswego Port Authority	1955
Brooklyn Sports Center Authority	1956
Higher Education Assistance Corporation	1957
New York State World War Memorial Authority	1957
East Hudson Parkway Authority	1960
New York State Housing Finance Agency	1960
Adirondack Mountain Authority	1960
New York State Job Development Authority	1961
New York State Atomic Research and Space Development Authority (Energy Research Development Authority)	1962
Manhattan and Bronx Surface Transit Operating Authority	1962
State University Construction Fund	1962
Mental Hygiene Facilities Inpatient Fund	1963
Metropolitan Commuter Transportation Authority (Metropolitan Transportation Authority)	1965
Long Island Rail Road	1966
Niagara Frontier Transportation Authority	1967
Battery Park City Authority	1968
United Nations Development Corporation	1968
Urban Development Corporation	1968
Rochester-Genesee Regional Transportation Authority	1969
Environmental Facilities Corporation	1970
State of New York Mortgage Agency	1970
Capital District Transportation Authority	1970
Central New York Transportation Authority	1970
New York Municipal Bond Bank Agency	1972
Medical Care Facilities Finance Agency	1973
Municipal Assistance Corporation	1975
Project Finance Agency	1975

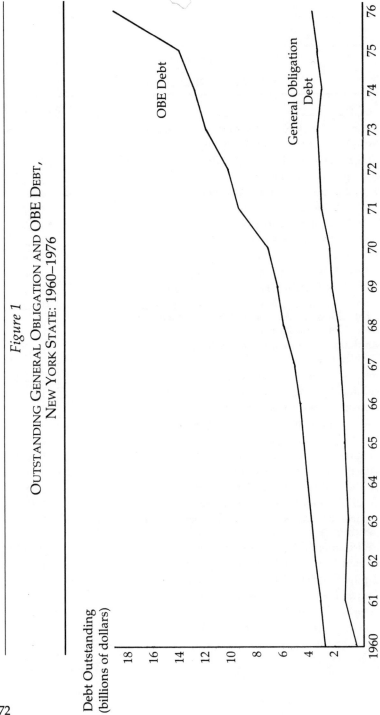

Figure 1

OUTSTANDING GENERAL OBLIGATION AND OBE DEBT,
NEW YORK STATE: 1960–1976

Debt Outstanding
(billions of dollars)

OBE Debt

General Obligation
Debt

Table 12

Revenues, Expenditures, Debt, and State Subsidies of Selected New York OBEs: 1980
(thousands of dollars)

OBE by Function	Total Revenues	Operating Expenses	Debt Service Requirements	Capital Program Expenditures	Bonds and Notes Outstanding	State Appropriations in Support of OBEs
BRIDGE, TUNNEL AND HIGHWAY						
Buffalo and Fort Erie Bridge	4,750	4,100	277	1,197	2,125	—
Lake Champlain Bridge Commission	633	301	—	333	—	700
New York State Bridge Authority	9,573	4,507	1,800	4,120	19,265	5,696
Ogdensburg Bridge and Port Authority	1,440	1,264	91	333	1,346	725
Thousand Islands Bridge Authority	3,279	2,343	549	194	500	—
Triborough Bridge and Tunnel Authority	249,800	56,400	29,600	6,128	231,000	—
Thruway Authority	160,500	114,211	40,156	3,347	606,037	—
ECONOMIC DEVELOPMENT						
Job Development Authority	17,606	1,440	15,396	5,737	135,658	—

Table 12 cont.

OBE by Function	Total Revenues	Operating Expenses	Debt Service Requirements	Capital Program Expenditures	Bonds and Notes Outstanding	State Appropriations in Support of OBEs
United Nations Development Corporation	19,959	11,605	3,482	4,100	55,682	—
Urban Development Corporation	107,506	33,913	95,547	106,100	995,763	81,491
ENERGY AND ENVIRONMENT						
Energy Research Development Authority	11,418	9,905	712	575	136,325	17,050
Environmental Facilities Corp.	2,874	1,872	1,002	—	36,198	3,552
Power Authority	956,500	738,100	333,400	114,700	2,573,901	—
HOUSING AND FINANCE						
Battery Park City Authority	10,086	3,865	14,279	10,734	392,630	4,950
Dormitory Authority	233,342	8,438	224,904	201,289	2,593,912	438,119
Housing Finance Agency	478,454	5,852	461,219	135,966	5,692,894	369,799
Medical Care Facilities Finance Agency	25,981	433	24,469	224	225,355	—

Table 12 cont.

OBE by Function	Total Revenues	Operating Expenses	Debt Service Requirements	Capital Program Expenditures	Bonds and Notes Outstanding	State Appropriations in Support of OBEs
Mortgage Agency	30,000	600	27,000	—	512,905	—
Municipal Assistance Corp. for the City of New York	598,055	6,415	591,640	—	6,516,198	—
Project Finance Agency	38,840	275	19,863	—	237,630	—
PORT DEVELOPMENT						
Albany Port District Comm.	1,116	1,130	453	3,396	2,183	6,323
Port Authority of New York and New Jersey	691,600	428,600	164,100	187,000	2,010,867	—
Port of Oswego Authority	1,050	900	75	300	—	934
Waterfront Commission of New York Harbor	5,984	5,984	—	—	—	—
REGIONAL TRANSPORTATION						
Capital District Transportation Authority	15,512	13,706	100	3,000	—	4,994
Central New York Regional Transportation Authority	11,784	11,765	—	980	1,000	4,183

Table 12 cont.

OBE by Function	Total Revenues	Operating Expenses	Debt Service Requirements	Capital Program Expenditures	Bonds and Notes Outstanding	State Appropriations in Support of OBEs
Metropolitan Transportation Authority	612,200	597,500	4,271	102,737	—	284,184
Metropolitan Suburban Bus Authority	27,600	27,600	—	—	—	—
New York City Transit Authority	1,682,700	1,652,400	11,000	400,000	43,610	764,105
Niagara Frontier Transportation Authority	39,496	36,964	1,500	99,534	—	94,385
Rochester Genesee Regional Transportation Authority	19,931	18,731	—	1,506	—	6,097
GRAND TOTAL	6,069,569	3,801,119	2,066,885	1,393,530	23,023,924	2,087,287

SOURCE: New York State, *1980–81 Budget*, appendix, table 4.

activity by New York State's OBEs, although the data are incomplete and do not list all statewide authorities. Given these data constraints, Table 12 shows that total expenditure of OBEs in 1980 were at least $7.2 billion, which is nearly 50 percent of the $15 billion in on-budget state spending for that year. The debt outstanding provides a more ominous picture. At $23 billion, the outstanding debt of OBEs is over five times that of the state government itself. And it is getting larger.

Further Financial Gimmickry

The moral obligation bond is just one of the tricks the Governor had up his sleeve to subvert constitutional borrowing constraints. Another gimmick which has come to be widely emulated by many other governments, both state and local, is the lease-purchase agreement.

When Rockefeller strolled into the governor's mansion in Albany, he realized that his surroundings were shabby, at best. With typically unbridled enthusiasm, he declared his immediate goal to make Albany "the most spectacularly beautiful seat of government in the world."[22] The voters would have nothing to do with spending over $2 billion to glorify the quarters of state politicians. But such concerns were of no consequence. Rockefeller arranged for Albany County to borrow the money, construct the buildings, and rent them to the state under a lease-purchase agreement. The state would pay rent over a 40-year period, at which time the state would obtain title to the buildings. It worked like a charm. Investors lent Albany County the money since the state was, in effect, underwriting the projects through its rental payments. With no-holds-barred construction strategy, two million square feet of marble, handpicked by the Governor, was used to construct numerous office buildings, all connected by a five-level underground plaza. The construction costs for what came to be known as "Rocky's Edifice Complex" were about five times greater than the cost for other buildings in the Albany area. Upon completion of this whirlwind construction project in 1973, the governor gratifyingly declared that, "If there is anything more satisfying than dedicating a new building, it is dedicating eight new buildings."[23]

The lease-purchase arrangement soon became the second barrel of Rockefeller's double-barrelled assault on state spending, and was used quite frequently to finance additional subsidized housing. The Gover-

[22]The following is discussed in McClelland and Magdovitz, pp. 234–36.

[23]M. Kramer and S. Roberts, *I Never Wanted to be Vice President of Anything!: An Investigative Biography of Nelson Rockefeller* (New York: Basic Books, 1976), as quoted in McClelland and Magdovitz, p. 235.

nor boasted of being "innovative" in employing the lease-purchase arrangement in the following statement:

> I was unable to obtain public approval of State bond issues to finance low-income housing. We therefore devised an innovative approach whereby the state can lease up to 50 percent of the apartments in a middle-income project to rent them to low-income families on a subsidy basis.[24]

As should be clear by now, the words "entrepreneurship" and "innovation," to the politician, are meant to convey not one's ability to benefit the voters, but one's ability to benefit in spite of them.

Other Statewide OBEs in the United States

Off-budget enterprises exist in every state and provide a variety of services such as airports, building construction, highways, industrial subsidizations, ports, toll bridges, mass transit, housing and urban renewal, student loans, parks, power, waterways, parking, atomic energy and space exploration research, marketing, and many others.

In one area, that of higher educational facilities, there has been a rapid proliferation of OBEs during the past two decades which, in retrospect, have grossly overinvested in educational facilities. During the 1960s, many educational "experts" were predicting continued increases in student enrollments and tuition income and warned that existing facilities would soon become outdated and overcrowded with the post-war "baby boom" generation coming of college age. The initial expansion during the 1960s was financed almost entirely by voter-approved general obligation borrowing. Between 1961 and 1971, the volume of tax-exempt bonds for higher education facilities increased from less than $170 million (almost entirely in state general-obligation debt) to more than $1.3 billion, over $1 billion of which was in the form of revenue bonds.[25] Eleven states created OBEs to make long-term loans to public and private colleges and universities during that period, and today every state issues revenue bonds for educational facilities, primarily dormitories and other buildings. Some states give public universities themselves the power to sell revenue bonds to finance their facilities, while others create separate off-budget entities such as the California Educational Facilities Corporation, the Indiana Educational

---

[24]"Analysis of the Philosophy and Public Record of Nelson A. Rockefeller, Nominee for Vice President of the United States, House Committee on the Judiciary, U. S. Congress," October 1974, p. 20.

[25]Annmarie Walsh, *The Public's Business* (Cambridge, Mass.: MIT Press, 1980), p. 164.

Facilities Authority, the Tennessee State School Bond Authority, the Pennsylvania State Public School Building Authority, the Wisconsin State Agencies Building Corporation, the Alabama Educational Authority, and many others.[26] Both lease-back and moral obligation bond techniques have been widely used to evade voter resistance to the rates of growth in educational spending desired by state politicians and educational administrators.

Despite the forecasts of the experts, student enrollments slowed during the 1970s and many students moved off campus in response to increased dormitory user fees. Consequently, there now exists a glut of unused dormitories and some colleges have gone bankrupt. Nevertheless, the costs of the unused facilities remain in the form of debt repayments, and are borne by students, parents, and taxpayers generally in the form of state and federal subsidies to education. Clearly, the use of revenue bonds to finance educational facilities has allowed state politicians to ignore voter preferences and to subsidize a small fraction of the population—students, university professors and administrators—at the expense of the general public. Requiring voter approval of bond issues would have at least limited this negative-sum activity and would have limited the financial strain facing state governments today.

Another type of off-budget enterprise which has proliferated at the state (and local) levels of government in recent years is the "sports authority." A 1976 *Bond Buyer* survey identified 44 cities planning new sports, civic, or convention centers, and dozens of new stadiums have been built in the past 20 years, financed with revenue bonds, after private capital markets had deemed them unworthy investments.[27] In this case, the bankers who refused to lend *private* entrepreneurs the money to finance such projects were apparently correct in their judgment. Even though various stadiums throughout the country take in revenues from many sources, including rents, concessions, parking fees and so on, there is not a single publicly owned stadium in the country that is self-supporting, and half do not even meet their operating expenses, let alone debt service.[28] Thus, OBEs have been used by state governments to force the *indirect* taxpayer support for projects which the private capital markets and voters had previously rejected,

[26]*Moody's Municipal and Government Manual* lists dozens of statewide educational building authorities (OBEs) which are active today.

[27]A. Bautzer, "Nation Experiences Boom in Costly Sports Facilities," *Weekly Bond Buyer*, May 6, 1974.

[28]Walsh, p. 140. The following is based on Walsh's discussion.

all to the benefit of various special interests such as politicians, construction firms and unions, investment bankers, and sports promoters.

One of the most-publicized sports facilities has been New Jersey's Meadowlands Stadium, built by the off-budget New Jersey Sports and Exposition Authority. The Meadowlands Stadium was constructed after exceptionally intense opposition by voters, who refused to guarantee debt for the venture, and by various other groups. Opponents made the arguments that: the project would establish paramutuel horse racing without voter consent, as required by the state's constitution; the sale of revenue bonds subverts constitutional debt limitations; state funds would be used to subsidize the operation, again in violation of the state's constitution; providing facilities for a private sports arena did not justify the taking of private property; the deal would illegally use public funds to subsidize a private firm (the New York Giants); and the stadium would provide unfair competition for private competitors. For example, Monmouth Park Race Track sued on the grounds that it pays 9.15 percent of its paramutuel pools to the state, while the Sports Authority's track pays only five percent.

In the courts, these arguments were all ignored, even though they were acknowledged as true. The judge justified these actions by citing Plato on the "profound moral force of sports" and cited the "contributions of ping-pong to rapprochement with Red China."[29] In the spring of 1973, the Sports Authority was authorized by the legislature to sell standard revenue bonds, but because of the poor revenue-generating record of sports arenas, the Authority had difficulty selling them. Moody's even refused to give the bonds any rating at all. The "solution" to this problem was to obtain a moral obligation pledge from the state. Even on the basis of the moral obligation pledge, Moody's gave the bonds its lowest rating, Baa, for institutional investment. Local politicians in the Meadowlands area who opposed the project sued the Sports Authority in federal court, but the courts upheld the Authority's position. Thus, a project that costs hundreds of millions of dollars, and is recognized by bankers, investors, voters, and local politicians alike to be in a category of known money losers, was forced upon the taxpayers of New Jersey by the State Sports and Exposition Authority and defended by the courts on what is best described as very shaky logic. Just as New York State's experiences with the HFA and UDC have spawned hundreds of similarly organized OBEs in other states, these precedents are likely to signal to other states that economically

[29]*New Jersey Sports and Exposition Authority* vs. *McCrane*, 119 N.J. 427 (1971).

80

inefficient, but politically profitable, investments in sports arenas and convention centers are possible after all, if only placed off-budget.

In many ways, New York State has served as a prototype for many other states. There has been a proliferation of state housing agencies in the past 20 years, and an association of HFAs has set its own Washington lobby. The Council of State Governments, comprised of state-level politicians and bureaucrats across the country, actively encourages the use of OBEs as a means of being more "flexible" in light of voter-imposed spending constraints. In a 1970 survey of statewide authorities, the Council concluded that:

> Constitutional debt limits are still the rule, not the exception. Technology continues to expand the area for delivery of government services. Complex interrelationships between government agencies at different levels require administrative flexibility; the authority device may be less rigid than the usual government agency.[30]

Translating from bureaucratese, it is the official position of the state-level political decision-makers that voter demands for fiscal restraint should be ignored by placing spending and borrowing off-budget. Unfortunately, New York is in no way a special case.

The overall magnitude of the activities of statewide OBEs in the United States is difficult, if not impossible to gauge, since many states do not even maintain data or information of any type on the activities of OBEs. Some light can be shed, however, on the volume of OBE activity across states by monitoring the volume of nonguaranteed debt issued in the securities markets, in which OBEs are major participants. Table 13 lists the long-term nonguaranteed state government debt, by state, for 1962, 1972, and 1977. In 1977, of total state government debt outstanding of $87.2 billion, $44.3 billion, or approximately 51 percent, was the nonguaranteed debt of OBEs. Nine states—Arizona, Arkansas, Colorado, Indiana, Iowa, Kansas, Nebraska, South Dakota, and Wyoming—actually do not permit voter approval of debt and issued a total of $1.8 billion in nonguaranteed debt in 1977.

As shown in the previous chapter (Table 8), there has been an increase in the proportion of total debt comprised of the nonguaranteed variety from 18.5 percent in 1950 to 55.9 percent in 1978. After an average annual increase in nonguaranteed debt as a percent of total debt of .3 percentage points from 1960 to 1977, the proportion increased by 51.1 percentage points from 1977 to 1978. This acceleration in the use of

---

[30]Council of State Governments, *State Public Authorities* (Washington, D.C.:CSG, 1970), p. 26. This document also lists selected OBEs state by state.

Table 13

LONG-TERM NONGUARANTEED STATE GOVERNMENT DEBT, BY STATE: 1962, 1972, 1977
(thousands of dollars)

State	1962 Amount	1962 Percent of Total Debt	1972 Amount	1972 Percent of Total Debt	1977 Amount	1977 Percent of Total Debt
Alabama	232,491	81.4	738,452	88.1	885,255	88.8
Alaska	—	—	116,366	32.8	358,275	40.3
Arizona	18,665	99.9	89,248	100.0	101,064	100.0
Arkansas	37,416	38.5	110,734	98.9	140,437	100.0
California	182,373	6.6	772,214	11.8	1,006,978	15.0
Colorado	64,823	100.0	120,151	100.0	197,266	100.0
Connecticut	346,900	40.0	273,784	13.6	764,001	24.1
Delaware	15,190	7.3	93,541	19.8	332,870	44.9
Florida	412,469	100.0	1,121,757	100.0	1,569,688	78.4
Georgia	438,339	99.9	984,344	99.9	899,685	70.9
Hawaii	87,532	42.6	257,719	33.0	302,732	20.6
Idaho	4,893	75.0	35,973	94.8	49,782	97.9
Illinois	468,991	64.0	1,278,601	73.6	2,252,380	58.0
Indiana	439,795	99.9	566,246	100.0	577,569	100.0
Iowa	16,001	33.5	111,256	94.5	123,951	100.0
Kansas	186,219	90.6	214,581	100.0	402,972	100.0
Kentucky	437,750	79.3	1,408,769	77.8	1,709,324	83.8

Table 13 cont.

State	1962 Amount	1962 Percent of Total Debt	1972 Amount	1972 Percent of Total Debt	1977 Amount	1977 Percent of Total Debt
Louisiana	103,901	26.8	547,033	48.6	466,010	26.4
Maine	85,154	61.3	51,199	18.7	289,208	51.3
Maryland	455,825	63.2	548,082	38.5	984,375	32.3
Massachusetts	559,281	37.5	694,710	31.8	1,345,153	29.6
Michigan	819,045	96.8	882,480	73.9	1,150,668	60.9
Minnesota	26,217	12.6	82,179	13.0	450,130	37.6
Mississippi	108,653	49.4	215,327	40.5	84,087	10.4
Missouri	27,617	31.4	110,795	79.7	361,361	82.0
Montana	49,104	91.4	94,840	99.9	93,992	92.7
Nebraska	19,783	100.0	83,176	100.0	59,297	100.0
Nevada	2,020	47.7	21,978	39.9	18,207	33.5
New Hampshire	1,430	1.6	19,424	12.5	118,280	34.6
New Jersey	433,391	47.0	1,127,130	47.6	2,274,781	57.5
New Mexico	42,799	68.9	123,879	88.5	186,932	88.2
New York	1,627,027	50.8	5,020,763	63.2	14,978,872	80.1
N. Carolina	16,416	6.3	111,972	20.8	173,957	21.6
N. Dakota	9,592	62.8	40,998	73.2	52,241	77.6
Ohio	744,855	83.3	1,009,729	48.3	1,079,156	35.2
Oklahoma	254,621	78.5	567,554	75.3	762,795	81.4

Table 13 cont.

State	1962		1972		1977	
	Amount	Percent of Total Debt	Amount	Percent of Total Debt	Amount	Percent of Total Debt
Oregon	71	—	—	—	19,065	.8
Pennsylvania	1,184,706	80.1	2,455,801	57.9	2,376,704	38.2
Rhode Island	6,821	6.4	78,593	22.8	364,442	57.1
S. Carolina	62,437	24.0	246,565	46.4	781,140	60.8
S. Dakota	8,752	100.0	39,629	100.0	218,441	100.0
Tennessee	9,651	7.0	209,383	38.2	404,604	36.9
Texas	190,728	44.4	655,168	48.8	1,239,076	58.3
Utah	19,551	100.0	56,607	58.6	60,536	41.6
Vermont	2,370	4.4	91,143	28.2	201,365	44.3
Virginia	203,982	96.4	279,410	80.0	715,761	94.6
Washington	428,455	88.4	837,891	85.4	292,551	20.7
West Virginia	173,711	59.9	331,995	48.4	456,824	34.7
Wisconsin	115,483	100.0	396,606	49.5	463,978	27.7
Wyoming	13,409	100.0	38,180	100.0	73,279	100.0

SOURCE: U.S. Department of Commerce, Bureau of the Census, *Census of Governments*, 1962, 1972, 1977.

nonguaranteed debt is likely to have been stimulated by the tax revolt of the 1970s, which came to a head in 1978 with the passage of Proposition 13, although more complete data are necessary before judgment is passed.

In any event, these data clearly show that statewide OBEs are quite active in each of the 50 states, conduct *all* of the borrowing in nine states, and on an aggregate level are responsible for more than half of all state government debt outstanding. These data have ominous implications for the American taxpayer: The machinery is now in place and operating on a wide scale that will thwart, to a large extent, any attempts at constitutional constraints on state-level taxing, borrowing, and spending as long as the off-budget mechanisms are used.

A rough approximation of the expenditures, as well as the debt, of all statewide OBEs can be made even though expenditure data are not readily available. The average state spent approximately one-fourth of the on-budget expenditures of New York State in 1979.[31] If one assumes that *off-budget* spending, on average, is also about one-fourth of that in New York, then—given that off-budget spending in New York State was near $8 billion[32] in 1980—total off-budget spending by state-level OBEs nationwide is estimated to be approximately $106 billion for that year. This would put *total* state government expenditure at about $249 billion in 1980—fully 74 percent higher than the $143 billion in on-budget spending.[33]

Recourse to the Courts: Who Protects the Taxpayer?

The taxpayers of New York State have not, of course, been completely bamboozled by the state's OBEs—there have been continual attempts by groups of taxpayers to challenge the legitimacy of constitutional neglect and subversion by politicians. For over a century, however, New York courts have ruled that "a citizen-taxpayer, who cannot show any direct or personal injury, lacks standing to challenge the allegedly unconstitutional expenditure of state moneys."[34] In short, the taxpayer who takes the state's politicians, who appoint the state's judges, to court for violating the constitution is without legal recourse.

[31]Tax Foundation, *Facts and Figures on Government Finance* (Washington, D.C.: Tax Foundation, Inc., 1979), p. 167.

[32]Table 12 shows $7.2 billion, but only lists 31 of the more than 40 statewise OBEs.

[33]Advisory Commission on Intergovernmental Relations, *Significant Features of Fiscal Federalism: 1980–81* (Washington, D.C.: ACIR, 1981), p. 12.

[34]McClelland and Magdovitz, p. 282, discuss the role of the courts in defending the moral-obligation mechanism.

There have been three skirmishes in the New York courts over the legitimacy of moral obligation bonds issued by OBEs. The first came in 1963 when, by a vote of four to three, the state supreme court upheld the notion that taxpayers could not challenge the legitimacy of the state's fiscal operations. By 1975, however, things had changed. An individual named Leon Wein sued the City of New York and the state for violating the state constitution by issuing moral obligation bonds, and won. Wein decided to test the constitutionality of New York City's newly created Stabilization Reserve Corporation (SRC). The court ruled that the issuance of moral obligation bonds by the SRC violated "both the letter and the spirit of the constitution," the judge having stated that "the SRC and other techniques for debt ceiling avoidance erode the principle of constitutional supremacy."[35] The supremacy of the state constitution did not last long, however, for just a few months later the Court of Appeals reversed this ruling by a four to three vote, and held that moral obligation debt did *not* violate the constitution. Thus, a signal was sent out to politicians everywhere that, in effect, constitutional debt restrictions are meaningless, and that the courts are ready to back it up if need be. Perhaps the best the taxpayer can hope for is that the American tradition, started with the Boston Tea Party and continued up through the case of Wein vs. New York City, will at least place some constraints on the seemingly unbridled spending habits of politicians. The enforcement of constitutional provisions remains one of the truly critical issues of our time.

Summary

At the state level of government, New York is by far the leader in off-budget spending, largely due to the exuberance of Nelson Rockefeller. New York State's constitutional debt limits have become a farce, with off-budget borrowing exceeding on-budget, voter-approved borrowing by a multiple of six. One OBE alone, the Housing Finance Agency, now has more debt outstanding (50 percent more) than the entire guaranteed debt of New York State, and the ability of the state's taxpayers to finance that debt is rapidly waning, given that high levels of taxation have led to a migration away from the state of both individuals and industries. There is good reason for the taxpayers of New York State to become alarmed over this situation, for despite the state's near-default in 1975, moral obligation borrowing remains unrestricted by law. It is quite bothersome, from the perspective of the taxpayer,

[35]Ibid., p. 287.

that a special commission established by Governor Hugh Carey in 1975, after describing in great detail the monumental failures of the state's off-budget enterprises and their proclivity toward bankruptcy, recommended in the final pages of its 285-page report that "there is good reason . . . to create . . . new authorities without delay. . . . New agencies, unburdened by the past, are essential and, therefore, recommended by the Commission."[36] This advice is not unlike telling someone dying of cirrhosis of the liver that what is needed is more alcohol, without delay. Both types of advice, one would think, would lead to a more rapid death.

The proclivity of politicians to routinely avoid constitutionally imposed spending and borrowing constraints is by no means peculiar to New York State. As shown here, statewide OBEs exist in each state, are responsible for over half of all state government borrowing, and are estimated to spend over $100 billion annually, which constitutes nearly half of total on- and off-budget state government spending. Thus, a very large segment of state government is beyond the direct control and scrutiny of taxpayers and is likely to grow even larger as pressures for fiscal restraint mount.

Although statewide OBEs have been quite active, to say the least, local governments in every state of the union have also created thousands of OBEs, including over 2,500 in Pennsylvania alone. The activities of local OBEs deserve closer scrutiny, which is the objective of the next chapter.

[36]New York State Moreland Act Commission, p. 285.

V. Off-Budget Activities of Local Government

Off-Budget Enterprises in Pennsylvania

Just as New York has the largest collection of statewide OBEs, its nearest neighbor, Pennsylvania, is by far the most active state in terms of off-budget spending and borrowing at the local level of government, with nearly 2,500 OBEs in operation. Local and state politicians in Pennsylvania have played a major role in developing off-budget mechanisms that have served as benchmarks for off-budget operations at the local level of government nationwide. A survey is given of the off-budget local public sector nationwide to show that OBEs exist in each state, dominate the municipal bond market, and, most annoyingly from the taxpayer's perspective, have enabled local politicians to respond to the tax revolt of the 1970s by placing billions of dollars of spending and borrowing off-budget and beyond the purview of recently enacted constitutional and statutory taxing and spending limits. Finally, two examples are given—New York City's bankruptcy in 1975, and the Washington Public Power Supply System's scrapping of two partially completed nuclear power plants costing billions of dollars—which show off-budget subversions of constitutional constraints on spending and borrowing have led to financial disaster for the taxpayers of New York and Washington State. One can only conclude that more of the same is in store for the nation's taxpayers as long as politicians practice the budgetary magic of off-budget enterprise.

During the late 19th and early 20th centuries, profligate borrowing practices by local governments in Pennsylvania led to frequent financial crises and defaults on debt payments.[1] As lenders and taxpayers became more suspicious of public borrowing, the state legislature was induced to impose severe restrictions on municipal borrowing by limiting it to seven percent of assessed property valuation. Pennsylvania voters were hopeful that their constitution could be used to constrain the irrespon-

---

[1] The following is found in D. Schlosser, *Municipal Authorities in Pennsylvania* (Harrisburg: State Department of Community Affairs, 1977).

sible borrowing practices of local politicians, but in 1935 the state legislature passed the Municipal Authorities Act, which exempted "government-owned corporations" from municipal debt restrictions. Numerous OBEs were soon created to finance school buildings, airports, parking lots, recreation centers, court houses, marketing, shipping, and transportation terminals, businesses, subways, bridges, tunnels, highways, parks and playgrounds, lakes, sewer systems, landfills, steam heating plants, flood control projects, hospitals and health care centers, industrial development subsidies, and other items. Local governments were no longer effectively constrained by the immediate wishes of the voters or by the intent of the state constitution.

In the late 1940s, Pennsylvania voters began pressuring their state representatives for limits on local property taxes. As a result, statutory property tax rate limits were enacted in 1949 which applied to cities, boroughs, townships, and school districts. The immediate response of local politicians and bureaucrats was to intensify the use of the off-budget mechanisms. The number of "municipal corporations" created tripled in 1950, and the amount of nonguaranteed bonds issued increased by 465 percent, from $11.5 million to $65 million in just one year. Thirty-four "school building authorities" alone were formed in 1950 compared to a total of 14 in the preceding 15 years. The amount of nonguaranteed debt issued by school building authorities increased by 583 percent in that year, from $2 million to $11.8 million. As seen in Table 14, by 1980 the number of OBEs in Pennsylvania had risen to 2,376, with $7.1 billion in debt outstanding, more than twice the amount of "full faith and credit" local debt outstanding.[2] As of 1980, over half of the total local debt outstanding in Pennsylvania was therefore not approved by and was beyond the control and scrutiny of taxpayers.

The lease-back arrangement is quite prevalent in Pennsylvania, as in New York, and local politicians there have used this mechanism to further evade any statutory or constitutional restrictions on their powers. For example, the Municipal Authorities Act does not specify that municipal governments may create lease-back electric power authorities. Local politicians have easily evaded this restriction by creating lease-back *water* authorities, selling their existing water systems to them, and using the proceeds of the sale to expand municipally owned electric power systems. Furthermore, many municipalities sell existing facilities to specially created OBEs and then lease them back simply to place them off-budget and beyond the view of the voters.

[2]Ibid.

Table 14

NUMBER AND BONDED INDEBTEDNESS OF OBEs IN PENNSYLVANIA, BY TYPE, JANUARY 1, 1980
(thousands of dollars)

Type	Number	Projects	Original Bond Issues ($000s)	Outstanding Bonds ($000s)
School	726	743	5,605,570	2,785,806
Water	269	557	1,084,301	649,916
Sewer	655	964	2,597,068	1,449,827
Airport	34	36	83,470	18,855
Parking	119	130	218,924	134,941
Recreation	84	100	102,605	85,295
Solid waste	42	53	41,040	14,394
Health	59	61	2,012,078	1,860,217
Others	60	92	120,882	102,801
Multipurpose	328	–	–	–
Total	2,376	2,736	11,865,938	7,102,052

SOURCE: Pennsylvania Department of Community Affairs, *Municipal Authorities in Pennsylvania* (Harrisburg: Department of Community Affairs, 1982), p. 21.

In sum, local government in Pennsylvania is largely beyond the direct control of taxpayers, and has been since the early 1950s when OBEs began to proliferate in response to tax limitations imposed by the state's constitution. Although it now "leads the nation" in off-budget debt outstanding ($7.1 billion in 1980), other states are rapidly catching up.

Off-Budget Local Government in the United States

Off-budget enterprises have proliferated at the local level of government in the past two decades. Indeed, they are the only unit of local government that has increased in number because of school district consolidations and a relative decline in the growth of special taxing districts. There are now literally thousands of OBEs at the local level of government in the United States,[3] in addition to the nearly 2,500 in Pennsylvania alone. While it is impossible to assess accurately the total level of OBE activity at the local level of government, since many governments keep no record of the spending and borrowing of OBEs, it is possible to shed some light on the problem by inspecting the municipal bond market. As shown in Table 15, the nonguaranteed debt

[3]Annmarie Walsh, *The Public's Business* (Cambridge, Mass.: MIT Press, 1980).

Table 15

NONGUARANTEED LOCAL GOVERNMENT DEBT, BY STATE: 1962, 1972, 1977
(thousands of dollars)

State	1962 Amount	1962 Percent of Total Debt	1972 Amount	1972 Percent of Total Debt	1977 Amount	1977 Percent of Total Debt
Alabama	405,542	57.1	1,088,919	67.8	731,101	49.6
Alaska	35,791	31.1	104,372	27.7	154,851	42.1
Arizona	308,521	57.4	328,807	28.6	1,333,652	52.7
Arkansas	88,649	33.6	517,049	64.0	187,468	53.0
California	1,477,787	25.7	3,858,099	33.5	5,744,828	43.7
Colorado	120,737	19.5	301,722	25.2	679,690	38.1
Connecticut	145,910	18.4	149,186	11.8	139,982	11.0
Delaware	34,976	26.2	123,863	40.0	116,576	35.0
Florida	915,755	58.6	2,220,572	64.8	3,370,369	66.8
Georgia	350,871	45.0	929,602	52.1	1,780,494	69.2
Hawaii	37,875	28.1	47,532	18.3	27,998	11.9
Idaho	43,463	35.7	53,832	35.5	10,734	27.8
Illinois	1,216,912	36.5	1,810,965	36.2	2,537,885	43.2
Indiana	459,108	52.8	966,391	53.2	863,006	58.2
Iowa	90,612	19.9	342,280	36.0	192,534	32.9
Kansas	160,012	25.6	444,814	43.8	600,834	61.1

Table 15 cont.

State	1962 Amount	1962 Percent of Total Debt	1972 Amount	1972 Percent of Total Debt	1977 Amount	1977 Percent of Total Debt
Kentucky	261,915	45.5	837,267	58.8	976,686	60.3
Louisiana	265,879	23.8	946,403	41.1	829,194	43.5
Maine	41,149	34.7	31,494	14.4	29,234	19.9
Maryland	221,309	18.3	371,571	15.2	250,007	10.3
Massachusetts	373,349	29.8	296,957	10.8	287,827	10.3
Michigan	354,622	17.9	928,057	18.5	1,200,379	20.7
Minnesota	175,342	16.5	391,791	13.9	685,280	23.8
Mississippi	82,220	20.3	269,655	34.3	182,818	42.2
Missouri	312,716	31.3	989,653	42.7	838,069	43.2
Montana	49,104	91.4	94,840	99.9	93,992	92.7
Nebraska	437,363	70.1	1,049,142	72.0	978,505	76.4
Nevada	26,359	21.6	124,383	28.8	223,002	41.2
New Hampshire	12,691	14.2	29,227	12.3	36,180	21.6
New Jersey	580,372	32.0	834,936	24.2	1,530,592	34.8
New Mexico	81,623	38.8	111,845	38.0	70,904	32.9
New York	2,357,892	23.9	3,725,046	22.8	4,462,250	19.7
N. Carolina	84,747	12.1	248,603	18.9	235,684	19.8
N. Dakota	16,384	11.2	52,389	27.9	42,957	72.8

Table 15 cont.

State	1962		1972		1977	
	Amount	Percent of Total Debt	Amount	Percent of Total Debt	Amount	Percent of Total Debt
Ohio	459,436	18.1	1,324,571	33.8	1,728,039	40.2
Oklahoma	127,259	22.7	328,793	29.6	364,900	37.4
Oregon	93,519	25.7	299,453	35.3	439,969	46.6
Pennsylvania	1,775,523	54.7	3,225,476	56.0	5,757,646	62.8
Rhode Island	33,027	16.9	53,998	15.8	43,912	14.1
S. Carolina	104,391	42.9	359,572	47.3	272,301	40.6
S. Dakota	7,968	13.5	12,783	14.5	7,997	41.2
Tennessee	481,843	41.1	912,491	39.5	954,497	40.2
Texas	1,009,254	27.5	2,408,434	33.0	4,166,521	41.1
Utah	103,392	41.1	151,533	40.7	117,353	26.7
Vermont	3,197	6.7	8,646	6.7	—	—
Virginia	383,779	36.7	487,502	11.4	388,208	14.6
Washington	1,382,074	74.4	2,688,826	73.5	3,526,075	76.1
W. Virginia	95,013	50.6	162,422	60.2	146,133	66.7
Wisconsin	128,946	12.8	217,046	11.0	249,058	16.1
Wyoming	32,822	31.6	71,748	65.3	—	—

SOURCE: U.S. Department of Commerce, Bureau of the Census, *Local Government in Metropolitan Areas*, 1962, 1972, 1977, table 12.

of OBEs constitutes a sizable portion of the total local government debt outstanding in each of the 50 states, comprising approximately 40 percent of total long-term debt outstanding ($62.1 billion) in 1977. The ratio of nonguaranteed to total long-term local government debt outstanding increased steadily during the 1962–1977 period in all but a few states, and constituted over half of all outstanding debt in 13 states in 1977, including 76.1 percent in Washington State, 72.8 percent in North Dakota, and 76.4 percent in Nebraska. Partly as a response to various tax or spending limitation measures and citizen demands for fiscal restraint, the proportion of nonguaranteed debt increased dramatically in several states during the period: from 13.1 percent to 41.2 percent in South Dakota; from 25.7 to 46.6 percent in Oregon; from 18.1 to 40.2 percent in Ohio; from 11.2 to 72.8 percent in North Dakota; from 27.5 to 62.8 percent in Montana; and from 25.6 to 61.1 percent in Kansas, to present just a few examples.

With respect to the revenues, expenditures, and payrolls of local OBEs, there are some scattered data available, although they too are incomplete. The Department of Commerce collects some data on the activities of "special districts"—with and without taxing powers. Only the latter category falls into our definition of an OBE, however. The revenues, expenditures and payrolls of this particular Census Bureau designation of off-budget enterprises are shown below, by state, in Table 16. As shown there, the expenditures of local OBEs amounted to approximately $9.6 billion in 1977, with payrolls close to $2 billion. The average increase in expenditures over the 1967–77 period of 285 percent is nearly double the 145 percent increase in total local public expenditures during that time,[4] and over three times the 80 percent increase in municipal government expenditures.[5]

The Census Bureau also provides data on another category of OBE—"city-operated utilities"—of which 70 percent of the debt is nonguaranteed. If one assumes that 70 percent of the total expenditures listed in Table 17 are also those of OBEs, then another $7.5 billion would be added to the total expenditures of OBEs for 1977, bringing the grand total to approximately $17.1 billion for that year. The data in Table 17 also reveal that OBEs are dominant suppliers of water, electric power, and natural gas, but avoid investing in mass transit, and for good

[4]Tax Foundation, *Facts and Figures on Government Finance* (Washington, D.C.: Tax Foundation, Inc., 1981), p. 18.

[5]U.S. Department of Commerce, Bureau of the Census, *Finances of Municipalities and Township Governments* (Washington, D.C.: U.S. Government Printing Office, 1977).

Table 16

Revenues, Expenditures, and Payrolls of Local Public Authorities: 1967–1977

(millions of dollars)

State	Revenues			Expenditures			Payrolls		
	1967	1977	% Change 1967–77	1967	1977	% Change 1967–77	1967	1977	% Change 1967–77
U.S.	2069.2	7729.8	275	2499.3	9612.2	285	553.6	1999.8	261
Alabama	52.02	220.51	324	63.69	224.25	252	12.82	40.26	214
Arizona	54.94	.05	−100	57.20	.043	−100	15.80	.022	−100
Arkansas	9.93	38.31	286	22.43	35.07	56	1.47	5.216	258
California	50.85	182.03	258	65.71	199.93	204	14.64	49.94	241
Colorado	5.03	19.28	283	6.36	59.41	834	1.17	3.75	221
Connecticut	22.50	39.67	76	35.52	49.40	39	4.35	14.90	243
Delaware	16.30	20.53	26	37.48	18.70	−50	2.37	4.13	74
D.C.	10.75	625.35	5717	25.43	741.44	2815	3.77	70.33	1766
Florida	33.49	88.38	164	43.16	81.76	89	10.42	28.92	178
Georgia	123.95	905.43	630	139.97	124.54	−11	52.65	320.58	508
Hawaii	.006	.034	467	.007	.032	357	.002	.022	1000
Idaho	5.34	11.0	106	5.02	9.49	89	1.26	3.41	171
Illinois	229.99	516.33	124	246.52	532.41	116	112.69	252.27	124
Indiana	71.81	231.50	228	84.50	210.52	149	12.90	27.44	113
Iowa	1.98	9.08	359	1.51	7.53	399	.78	2.02	159

Table 16 cont.

State	Revenues			Expenditures			Payrolls		
	1967	1977	% Change 1967–77	1967	1977	% Change 1967–77	1967	1977	% Change 1967–77
Kansas	23.21	83.62	260	21.66	133.64	517	5.99	17.48	192
Kentucky	6.42	28.06	337	10.23	29.03	184	1.04	4.06	290
Louisiana	18.81	—	—	18.29	—	—	4.07	—	—
Maine	9.62	55.01	472	10.63	69.21	551	2.5	8.26	230
Maryland	3.91	63.63	1527	9.15	100.29	996	.7	16.85	2307
Massachusetts	121.92	438.84	260	129.85	538.64	315	53.76	176.49	228
Michigan	6.90	81.58	1082	8.37	86.99	939	1.71	19.47	1039
Minnesota	.51	.22	−57	1.07	.20	−81	0.28	0.03	−89
Mississippi	4.95	18.73	278	4.59	15.74	243	0.88	3.29	274
Missouri	44.60	168.55	278	52.86	155.38	194	3.95	33.49	748
Montana	2.36	8.08	242	2.11	7.33	247	0.72	2.72	277
Nebraska	162.08	486.07	200	162.53	777.46	378	31.17	69.55	123
Nevada	4.06	7.68	89	4.48	14.49	223	1.21	2.72	125
N. Hampshire	4.58	8.83	93	4.46	9.45	112	0.56	1.35	141
New Jersey	113.54	420.05	270	145.89	499.77	242	23.76	68.93	190
New Mexico	1.94	0.032	−98	1.81	0.061	−97	0.20	0.045	−77
New York	214.46	548.19	156	215.56	620.18	188	70.05	193.73	176
N. Carolina	14.96	152.16	917	29.44	171.61	483	2.16	55.40	2464

Table 16 cont.

State	Revenues			Expenditures			Payrolls		
	1967	1977	% Change 1967–77	1967	1977	% Change 1967–77	1967	1977	% Change 1967–77
N. Dakota	1.17	2.99	155	2.17	2.83	30	0.30	0.59	97
Ohio	33.66	140.18	316	52.45	154.05	194	9.47	41.20	335
Oklahoma	2.05	34.54	1585	3.81	38.72	916	0.42	5.84	1290
Oregon	7.97	29.88	275	8.99	36.61	307	2.34	7.98	241
Pennsylvania	312.21	1159.0	2712	406.78	1274.66	213	47.38	238.90	404
Rhode Island	6.66	17.15	157	6.72	17.09	154	1.51	4.80	218
S. Carolina	12.50	41.88	235	12.28	42.85	249	2.31	6.42	178
S. Dakota	0.80	4.83	504	1.01	8.30	722	.34	0.51	50
Tennessee	48.07	138.27	188	64.73	138.37	114	6.47	26.24	305
Texas	75.13	363.77	384	86.85	529.25	509	12.38	75.98	514
Utah	.84	.94	12	.69	.85	23	.15	.22	47
Vermont	.31	1.71	452	.94	4.49	378	.055	.36	554
Virginia	24.27	76.94	217	30.38	94.24	210	5.34	20.18	278
Washington	87.56	194.35	122	142.67	568.18	298	11.72	20.35	74
W. Virginia	5.10	28.9	467	7.64	33.23	335	.86	7.11	727
Wisconsin	.93	14.90	1502	1.50	20.07	1238	.14	2.20	1471
Wyoming	2.21	3.52	59	2.20	3.50	59	0.63	1.12	78

SOURCE: U.S. Dept. of Commerce, Bureau of the Census, *Census of Governments*, Vol. 4, *Finances of Special Districts* (Washington, D.C.: U.S. Government Printing Office, 1977).

Table 17

FINANCES OF CITY-OPERATED UTILITIES, BY TYPE: 1976–77
(thousands of dollars)

Item	Total	Water Supply	Electric Power	Transit	Gas Supply
Revenue	10,741,423	3,822,707	5,353,457	940,850	624,409
Expenditure	12,058,142	4,306,190	5,376,766	1,810,678	564,508
Current Operations	8,502,110	2,569,817	4,122,912	1,188,134	521,147
Salaries and Wages	2,701,747	1,084,508	586,676	966,304	64,259
Other	5,800,363	1,485,309	3,536,236	321,830	456,988
Capital Outlay	2,639,716	1,161,402	908,798	433,263	36,253
Construction	2,164,111	1,043,260	707,186	385,827	27,838
Other	475,605	218,142	201,612	47,436	8,415
Interest on Debt	916,316	474,971	345,056	89,281	7,008
Long-Term Debt					
Outstanding	19,043,120	10,261,494	6,417,451	2,213,325	150,850
Nonguaranteed	13,430,032	7,121,345	6,108,561	59,882	140,244
Full Faith and Credit	5,613,088	3,140,149	308,890	2,153,443	10,606

SOURCE: U.S. Dept. of Commerce, Bureau of the Census, *Census of Governments*, Vol. 4, *Finances of Municipalities and Townships* (Washington, D.C.: U.S. Government Printing Office, 1977).

reason. The expected user-fee revenues from the former three services are much more certain or reliable than are those for transit, given that there are so many easily adaptable substitutes for trains and buses compared to electric power, water, and gas. Like the Port Authority of New York and New Jersey, which has been chastised for years for investing in lucrative projects such as the World Trade Center rather than the perennial money loser[6]—government-owned mass transit—local politicians have followed suit in not devoting much of the capital raised by OBEs to finance mass transit facilities.

Overall, if one assumes that the level of spending by local OBEs had increased at the same rate as did new issues of the revenue bonds issued by OBEs from 1976 to 1980, then expenditures would have roughly doubled during that time to at least $35 billion in 1980.

Off-Budget Encouragement by the Federal Government

Federal sponsorship of OBEs at the local and state level of government has been widely felt and has been non-partisan ever since the early 1930s, when the Reconstruction Finance Corporation (RFC) and the Public Works Administration (PWA) were financed to subsidize OBEs by purchasing their revenue bonds. This federal initiative was quite successful at stimulating the growth of OBEs at the local and state levels of government. In Pennsylvania, over 50 OBEs were created between 1935 and 1942, about half of which received federal aid.[7] Between 1933 and 1935 New York State created 15 OBEs, three times the number created in the previous 12 years. By 1948 all but seven states had adopted enabling legislation for OBEs, and the amount of nonguaranteed debt increased rapidly, from near zero in 1937 to $151 million in 1938, and to $550 million in 1948, a 265 percent increase during that decade. By contrast, the voter-approved general obligation debt of state and local governments increased by 143 percent during the same period. In 1955, President Eisenhower actively advocated federal legislation to encourage local governments to create off-budget school building authorities that could ignore restrictive debt limits in order to build schools. The following quotation seems decidedly out of character for the president who condemned the Tennessee Valley Authority, a federal OBE and pet project of Franklin Roosevelt, as "creeping socialism":

[6]Walsh.

[7]Dun and Bradstreet, *Moody's Municipal and Government Manual* (New York: Dun and Bradstreet Co., 1981).

Many school districts cannot borrow to build schools because of restrictive debt limits. They need some other form of financing. Therefore, (this) proposal is designed to facilitate immediate construction of schools without local borrowing by the school district.

To expand school construction, several States have already created special statewide school building agencies. These can borrow advantageously, since they represent the combined credit of many communities. After building schools, the agency rents them to school districts. The local community under its lease gets a new school without borrowing.

I now propose the wider adoption of this tested method of accelerating school construction. Under this proposal the Federal Government would share with the States in establishing and maintaining for State school-building agencies an initial reserve fund equal to 1 year's payment on principal and interest.

The State School-building agency, working in cooperation with the State educational officials, would issue its bonds through the customary investment channels, then build schools for lease to local school districts. Rentals would be sufficient to cover the payments on principal and interest of the bonds outstanding . . . In time, the payments . . . would permit repayment of the initial Federal and State advances. When all its financial obligations to the agency are met, the local school district takes title to its building.[8]

Federal sponsorship of local OBEs remains strong for practical political reasons. Federal politicians wanting to dispense benefits upon their constituents to win votes quite naturally hesitate to require accompanying tax increases (which lose votes), as is the case with matching grants awarded to on-budget governmental agencies. From the perspective of the local politician, federal aid to OBEs is somewhat like manna from heaven, which can be used to benefit constituents through either increasing spending, holding taxes constant or reducing taxes, or holding spending levels constant, all at the expense of the general taxpaying public. So mutually advantageous is this arrangement to federal and local politicians that there are now dozens of federal aid programs which bypass general purpose, on-budget units of local government and distribute funds directly to OBEs.[9] The following list provides examples of such funding:

—Mass Transportation Loans established by the Housing Act of 1961

[8]Message from the President of the United States, H.R. Doc. No. 84, 84th Cong., 1st Sess. 3 (1955) as quoted in C. Robert Morris, "Evading Debt Limitations with Public Building Authorities: The Costly Subversion of State Constitutions," *Yale Law Journal* 68 (December 1958): 240–41.

[9]Advisory Commission on Intergovernmental Relations, *Regional Decision Making: New Strategies for Substate Districts* (Washington, D.C.: ACIR, 1973).

—Mass Transportation Demonstrations established by Section 303 of the Housing Act of 1961
—Public Housing established by the U.S. Housing Act of 1937, as amended
—Open Space Land Acquisition authorized under Title VII of the Housing Act of 1961
—Urban Renewal Projects authorized by Title I of the Housing Act of 1949, as amended
—Urban Renewal Demonstrations authorized by Section 314 of the Housing Act of 1954
—Public Facility Loans authorized by Title II of the Housing Amendments of 1955
—Advances for Public Works Planning established by Section 702 of the Housing Act of 1954, as amended
—Hospital and Medical Facilities Construction established by the Hospital Survey and Construction Act of 1946, as amended
—Waste Treatment Works authorized under Section 6 of the Federal Water Pollution Control Act of 1956, as amended
—Land for Recreation and Public Purposes authorized under the Recreation Act of 1926 (43 U.S.C. 869), as amended by the Recreation and Public Purposes Act of 1954
—Reclamation authorized under the federal reclamation laws

Through a virtual sea of federal aid programs, local OBEs now receive at least 30 percent of their revenues, on average, in the form of intergovernmental aid.[10] So anxious are federal politicians to distribute and local politicians to receive federal aid, that there are literally thousands of OBEs in existence which do nothing but collect federal grants! Stephens and Olson[11] discovered that there are at least 17,500 "toy governments" in the United States which do not employ a single full-time employee, but nevertheless receive millions of dollars in federal aid. There are another 4,000 or so local government entities with only one employee. As an indication of how extensive the practice of creating "toy governments" has been, Stephens and Olson report that when the first revenue-sharing checks were mailed out in late 1972, over 5,000 were returned "addressee unknown"!

[10]U.S. Department of Commerce, Bureau of the Census, *Financing Special Districts* (Washington, D.C.: U.S. Government Printing Office, 1977).

[11]G. Ross Stephens and Gerald W. Olson, *Pass-Through Federal Aid and Interlevel Finance in the American Federal System: 1957–1977*, Report to the National Science Foundation, NSF/APR 7700348, August 1, 1979.

The Off-Budget Response to the Tax Revolt of the '70s

The massive machinery of off-budget enterprise which exists at the local level of government was well prepared to meet the challenge of the taxpayer's revolt of the 1970s, in which numerous statutory and constitutional restrictions on the ability of local governments to tax and spend were imposed. Much to the taxpayer's dismay, the 1950 response of local governments in Pennsylvania to tax and spending limitation has proven to be the rule rather than the exception, for the tax revolt has yielded a similar response nationwide. This can be seen by first examining local governmental borrowing activity in five states which enacted tax or expenditure limitations on local governments during the early 1970s.[12] The five states, with the year in which tax/expenditure limits were enacted in parentheses, are: Indiana (1972), Kansas (1970), Minnesota (1972), Montana (1974), and Wisconsin (1973). Table 18 shows the amounts of nonguaranteed local government debt in these states in 1962, 1972, and 1978. In each state, both the amount of nonguaranteed debt and the ratio of nonguaranteed to total long-term local government debt increased substantially more during the 1972–78 period than during the 1962–72 period. The most dramatic increase occurred in Montana, where nonguaranteed debt increased by 494 percent between 1972 and 1978. The ratio of guaranteed to total long-term debt in Montana increased from 37 percent in 1972 to 70 percent in 1978. In both Wisconsin and Minnesota the ratio of nonguaranteed to total long-term local debt declined from 1962 to 1972, and then more than doubled in each state during the 1972–78 period. Indiana's nonguaranteed to total debt ratio remained approximately constant for 10 years, and then rose from 53 percent in 1972 to 68 percent six years later. On average, the amount of nonguaranteed local government debt in these five states increased by 249 percent between 1972 and 1978 (compared to an average 112 percent during the previous decade).

In comparison, those states which had enacted no restraints whatsoever on local government taxing and spending powers prior to 1977 experienced a much slower increase in the amount of nonguaranteed debt issued and had significantly lower nonguaranteed to total long-term debt ratios, as Table 19 shows. These states had an average nonguaranteed to total debt ratio of 26.7 percent in 1978 compared to 50.2 percent in the "tax-limitation" states. In addition, the ratio of nonguaranteed to total long-term debt increased, on average, by 5.6 per-

---

[12]Advisory Commission on Intergovernmental Relations, *State Limitations on Local Taxes and Expenditures* (Washington, D.C.: ACIR, 1977).

Table 18

NONGUARANTEED LOCAL GOVERNMENT DEBT IN INDIANA, KANSAS, MINNESOTA, MONTANA, WISCONSIN: 1962, 1972, 1978
(millions of dollars)

State	1962		1972			1978		
	Amount	% of Total	Amount	% Change 1962–72	% of Total	Amount	% Change 1972–78	% of Total
Indiana	459.1	52.8	966.4	110	53	1,957.6	103	68
Kansas	160.0	25.6	444.8	178	44	1,161.5	161	56
Minnesota	175.3	16.5	391.8	124	14	1,421.9	263	33
Montana	35.7	27.5	63.4	78	37	376.4	494	70
Wisconsin	128.9	12.8	217.1	68	11	705.0	225	24

SOURCE: *Compendium of Governmental Finances* (Washington, D.C.: Bureau of the Census, 1962, 1972) and *Moody's Municipal and Government Manual* (New York: Dun and Bradstreet Co., 1981).

Table 19

NONGUARANTEED LOCAL GOVERNMENT DEBT IN STATES WITHOUT TAX OR EXPENDITURE LIMITATIONS PRIOR TO 1977
(millions of dollars)

State	1962 Amount	1962 % of Total	1972 Amount	1972 % Change 1962–72	1972 % of Total	1978 Amount	1978 % Change 1972–78	1978 % of Total
Arkansas	88.6	34	517.0	574	64	650.6	26	60
California	1,477.8	26	3,858.1	161	34	6,152.3	59	43
Connecticut	145.9	18	149.2	2	12	309.0	107	20
Hawaii	37.9	28	47.5	25	18	33.4	–30	10
Maine	41.1	35	31.5	–23	14	29.2	–7	21
Massachusetts	373.3	30	296.9	–20	11	883.0	197	24
Tennessee	481.8	41	912.5	89	40	1,517.0	66	42
Vermont	3.2	7	8.6	169	7	22.6	163	19
Maryland	221.3	18	371.6	68	15	588.4	58	17
New Hampshire	12.7	14	29.2	130	12	41.3	41	11

SOURCE: *Compendium of Governmental Finances and Moody's Municipal and Government Manual.*

centage points in no-limit states and by 18 percentage points in tax-limit states during the 1972–78 period.

From this evidence it is clear that even though tax and expenditure limits may have reduced the growth of on-budget local expenditures in the five tax-limit states, billions of dollars of debt and expenditure have been placed off-budget through the OBE device.

Even though many consider the passage of California's Proposition 13 in June 1978 to be the beginning of the taxpayer revolt of the '70s, the tax revolt was simmering throughout the early 1970s. And, as shown below, so was the growth of the off-budget local public sector. The tax revolt has been gaining momentum at the local level of government throughout the past decade. Eleven states passed 18 different initiatives during the period from 1970 to 1973.[13] Only three spending restrictions were passed in 1974 and 1975, but the tax revolt began to intensify in 1975 when voters passed only 29 percent of the total amount of bond issues subject to referenda, compared to 62 percent in 1974.[14] The tax rebellion became much more pronounced in 1976. In 1976 and 1977, 11 states imposed tax or spending limits on local governments, followed by 16 more states in the following two years, including Proposition 13. Thus it appears that the tax revolt began in earnest in 1976, although it had been fermenting since 1970.

There is considerable evidence that the tax revolt has elicited a massive amount of off-budget spending and borrowing activity at the local level. Consider the ratios of nonguaranteed to guaranteed (NG/G) and negotiated to competitively bid (N/C) municipal security sales.[15] Nearly all guaranteed municipal securities are sold through competitive bids among a number of competing underwriters. By contrast, OBEs generally negotiate with a single underwriter. Throughout the 1970s there has been a continuous increase in both the NG/G and the N/C ratios. There was a sharp incease in the NG/G ratio beginning in 1976, with the intensification of the tax revolt. After an average yearly increase of about 19 percent for 10 years, the amount of nonguaranteed local debt issued in 1977 increased by 66 percent, from $17.2 to $28.6 billion, while sales of voter-approved guaranteed municipal debt had fallen from $18.2 billion in 1976 to $14.1 billion, increasing the NG/G ratio from .95 to 2.43.

[13]ACIR, *State Limitations on Local Taxes and Expenditures* (Washington, D.C.: ACIR, 1981).

[14]ACIR (1977), p. 74.

[15]Data on municipal security sales were obtained from Public Securities Association, *Statistical Yearbook of Municipal Finance* (New York: Public Securities Assoc., 1981).

The N/C ratio also rose sharply with the intensification of the tax revolt. After increasing by an average 27 percent per year from 1966 to 1974, the volume of negotiated municipal security sales increased by 52 percent from $6.9 billion to $10.6 billion in 1975. This is largely the result of the small percentage of guaranteed debt (29 percent) approved by voters during that year. Between 1975 and 1980, the volume of negotiated municipal security sales increased by 162 percent, from $10.6 to $27.8 billion, while competitively bid sales remained at approximately $19.5 billion. The N/C ratio rose from .42 in 1974 to 1.43 in 1980. Thus the tax revolt has incited a rapid increase in the growth of the off-budget local public sector, although this expansion may have levelled off since 1979.

As a final piece of evidence, consider the pattern of new issues of state and local government securities, by type, as shown in Table 20. The category "Special District/Statutory Authority" is the Census Bureau terminology for off-budget enterprise, and lists the nonguaranteed debt of OBEs at the local *and* state levels of government. Even though these data are incomplete, they nevertheless show a striking increase in OBE debt beginning, once again, in 1975. Since 1975, OBE debt has been the largest and fastest-growing type of state and local government debt issued. OBE debt increased by 172 percent between 1974 and 1980,

Table 20

NEW ISSUES OF STATE AND LOCAL GOVERNMENT SECURITIES:
1970–1979
(billions of dollars)

Item	1970	1972	1973	1974	1975	1976	1977	1978	1979
All Issues	18.2	23.7	24.0	24.3	30.6	35.3	46.8	48.6	43.5
Guaranteed	11.9	13.3	12.3	13.6	16.0	18.0	18.0	17.9	12.1
Nonguaranteed	6.1	9.3	10.6	10.2	14.5	17.1	28.7	30.7	31.3
Type of Issues									
State	4.2	5.0	4.2	4.8	7.4	7.1	6.4	6.6	4.4
Special District/ Statutory Authority	5.6	9.5	9.5	8.6	12.4	15.3	21.7	24.2	23.4
Municipalities, Counties, Town- ships	8.4	9.2	10.2	10.8	10.7	12.8	18.6	17.7	15.6

SOURCE: *Statistical Abstract of the U.S.* (Washington, D.C.: U.S. Bureau of the Census, 1980), p. 300.

while the voter-approved debt of municipalities, counties, and townships combined increased by 44 percent, and the guaranteed debt issued by state governments actually declined by nine percent. Overall, new issues of nonguaranteed debt continued to increase through 1979, although not as rapidly as during the 1974 to 1977 period, while guaranteed debt issues fell steadily from 1976 to 1979. The sharp decline in guaranteed debt from 1978 to 1979 is mainly responsible for the fact that *total* state and local debt issued fell in 1979 for the first time in 10 years. Thus, it appears that the tax rebellion elicited a dramatic increase in off-budget spending and borrowing in 1977, and continues to do so, but at a slower rate.

In summary, the data show that local and state politicians and bureaucrats have responded to the tax revolt by placing billions of dollars of debt and expenditure off-budget and beyond the control and scrutiny of the voters. Reports that the tax revolt has reduced the burden of taxation at the local level of government are therefore uncertain. Although data on property taxes may indeed show a relative slowdown, the true opportunity cost of government, as Friedman[16] asserted, is not measured by explicit taxes, but by government spending. And there is no conclusive evidence that local government spending has been reduced; its *rate* of growth may have been reduced somewhat, but much of it has merely been concealed.

Clearly, the spending and investment activities of local off-budget enterprises have had a large impact on the local public economy, and are growing rapidly. The implications for the taxpayer are ominous: A large and growing segment of the local public sector is substantially beyond the direct control, but not the pocketbooks, of the taxpayers, and OBEs can be expected to "mobilize" against any future taxpayer attempts at constitutional constraints on taxing and spending. Off-budget activities have placed a serious financial strain on local governments nationwide, have crowded out billions of dollars of private sector spending and investment, and have contributed to several financial debacles, most notably the bankruptcy of New York City and the state in 1975 and the scrapping of two partially completed nuclear power plants in Washington State in 1982.

Off-Budget Enterprise and the New York City Bankruptcy

On May 29, 1975, the government of New York City found itself, at its periodic city council meeting, in dire financial straits, to put it mildly.

[16]Milton Friedman, "The Limitations of Tax Limitation," *Policy Review* 5 (Summer 1978): 1–14.

In the next 30 days over $1 billion in bills would come due, and the city was flat broke. Furthermore, the city's credit rating was so poor that absolutely no one was willing to lend it that kind of money. The financial capital of the world had gone bankrupt, and only the eventual bail-out by the federal and state governments would save it or, more accurately, prolong the true day of reckoning. What had gone wrong? Basically, the city went under because constitutional constraints on government spending and borrowing were circumvented by the city politicians in order to finance a truly extraordinary increase in both welfare payments and payments to city employees. In short, the New York City financial disaster was caused by the insatiable appetite of local politicians for spending money on large and powerful interest groups, while deferring the costs of those transfers to future taxpayers via the mechanics of debt financing, even if it meant violating constitutional borrowing constraints. But in 1975 the bill for these illusions came due, and the city was unable to pay. As will be seen, OBEs played an important role in New York City's evasion of constitutional spending and debt limits, much in the spirit of state-level OBEs under the guidance of Nelson Rockefeller.

In the 10 years prior to New York City's financial collapse, operating expenditures rose by about $8.3 billion, of which approximately 27 percent is estimated to have gone for welfare spending and 43 percent for labor costs.[17] By fiscal year 1976, New York City was topping all other cities in welfare outlays per recipient, spending a total of over $5 billion.[18] The growth in welfare spending, which had increased from 12.3 percent of the city budget in 1961 to 22.6 percent in 1976, was caused, in part, by what economist Gordon Tullock calls "self-generating growth." High levels of welfare payments attracted more recipients to the New York City area—from Puerto Rico, depressed rural areas of the South, and elsewhere—who combined with the original recipients to lobby for ever-greater spending, which in turn attracted even more applicants for welfare. The end result of this process as of 1975 was a very generous welfare program whereby one-sixth of the population received some form of public assistance due to very broad eligibility requirements, one-fifth of the population was eligible for free health care under Medicaid, and the medical services provided were the most extensive in the nation.

[17]New York City Temporary Commission on City Finances, *An Historical and Comparative Analysis of Expenditures in the City of New York*, October 1976. These numbers should be taken with a grain of salt, since they originate from the New York City accounts.
[18]Ibid.

In addition to welfare spending, the rapid escalation of public employee wages and benefits also contributed to New York City's bankruptcy. The political power of the public employee unions in New York City is formidable. In addition to striking, which they have often done illegally, one author estimates that given that at least 49 out of every 1000 residents are city employees, and assuming each employee is married and can influence the vote of one relative or close friend, public employees constitute 30 percent of all eligible voters, or close to half of those likely to vote in an election.[19] The fact that public employees generally vote more frequently than the average citizen further enhances the political power of this voting bloc.[20]

This political power has led to high wages for New York City workers, but not exceptionally high when compared to other large cities. In fact, the Congressional Budget Office in 1976 concluded: "Considering that New York's cost of living—as measured by the Bureau of Labor Statistics intermediate family budget—is higher than all cities but that of Boston, its wages are not particularly out of line."[21]

What is, in fact, out of line is New York City employee fringe benefits, including retirement benefits, days off for giving blood, extra-long lunch periods, guaranteed rest periods, health and disability insurance, and so on. According to one estimate, the total cost of all fringe benefits added about 68 cents to every dollar paid out in wages in 1975, compared to about 35 cents for federal employees and 30 cents for private sector workers.[22] Pensions alone had grown from $261 million in 1961 to $1.3 billion in 1975, and were rising rapidly. Thus, the right to collective bargaining which was given to public employees and their unions in 1958 has resulted in only slightly abnormal wages, but extraordinarily high levels of fringe benefits. Between 1960 and 1970 there were a total of 216 statutes passed related to pension benefits for dozens of unions, including such liberal benefits as: the right to retire at half pay after 20 years of service; escalation of payments; calculation of retirement benefits on the basis of earnings during the last year of employment (which greatly increased the amount of overtime put in by potential retirees); and employee withdrawal from pension fund

[19]Edward Gramlich, "The New York City Fiscal Crisis: What Happened and What Is To Be Done?," *American Economic Review*, May 1976, pp. 415–29.

[20]For evidence of this, see James T. Bennett and William P. Orzechowski, "The Voting Behavior of Bureaucrats: Some Empirical Evidence," *Public Choice*, forthcoming, 1983.

[21]Congressional Budget Office, "The Causes of New York City's Fiscal Crisis," *Political Science Quarterly*, Winter 1976, p. 671.

[22]William E. Simon, *A Time for Truth* (New York: McGraw-Hill, 1978).

contributions.[23] The reason why this union assault on the taxpayers of New York took place, and why city politicians were so willing to allow it to take place, is straightforward. Granting wage increases gains an incumbent politician the support of the labor unions, but the *current* taxes required to pay the wage bill loses votes among non-union taxpayers. Giving in to only slightly above-average wages but extremely generous pension and fringe benefits garners the support of the unions without alienating the taxpayers quite as much, for the bill for the pension benefits comes due in future years—and by that time, political incumbents had hoped to be long gone, on to bigger and better things at the state or federal level. Unfortunately for New York City, the bills came due before most politicians anticipated, and were unpayable because of the heavy reliance on debt finance of current expenditures, much of which was conducted by off-budget enterprises.

The City of New York *is* subjected to state-imposed constitutional constraints on fiscal profligacy which, one would think, would help to avoid default and bankruptcy. The state constitution mandates a balanced budget, which precludes any borrowing to finance current expenses, and requires all municipal debt issues to be approved by the voters in referenda. In addition, there is a debt limit of 10 percent of the value of taxable real estate. As is the case with New York's state government, OBEs have been adopted as a means of routinely ignoring these constitutional constraints on New York City's ability to borrow and spend. Also, the debt restrictions have been evaded by a number of other techniques such as simply amending the constitution to exempt certain items from the limits, such as water supply facilities, docks, rapid transit facilities, low-rent housing, hospitals, and schools. Also excluded from the debt limit is short-term debt.

Perhaps the most lethal of all the financial gimmicks used to avoid constitutional spending constraints was the use of both OBEs and on-budget agencies to borrow to finance *current* expenditures. The constitutional requirement of a balanced budget was ignored by simply having the state legislature classify various current expenditures as capital expenditures by claiming that they have a "probable useful life" of 3–30 years! Examples include spending for vocational education (30 years); cleaning of buildings (10 years); assistance to residents eligible for public assistance (five years); conducting a special census (three years); and so on.[24] As shown in Table 21, the amount of borrowing for current

[23]New York City Temporary Commission.

[24]P. McLelland and A. Magdovitz, *Crisis in the Making* (Cambridge: Cambridge Press, 1981), p. 324.

Table 21
BORROWING FOR CURRENT EXPENSES IN NEW YORK CITY, FISCAL YEARS 1965–78

Fiscal Year	Total city capital budget funds ($ millions)	Borrowing for current expenses	
		Amount ($ millions)	% of city capital budget funds
1965	720	26	3.6
1966	590	57	9.7
1967	538	68	12.6
1968	673	68	10.0
1969	619	84	13.6
1970	800	151	18.9
1971	1,004	195	19.4
1972	1,162	226	19.4
1973	1,342	274	20.0
1974	1,359	564	41.5
1975	1,376	724	52.6
1976	1,445	697	48.2
1977	713	572	80.2
1978	865	608	70.3

SOURCE: Data provided by Citizens Budget Commission; reproduced in New York City Temporary Commission on City Finances, *The City in Transition: Prospects and Policies for New York*, Final Report (New York: Arno Press, 1978), p. 157.

expenses rose from only $26 million in 1965 to $724 million in 1975, the year of bankruptcy—an increase of 2,500 percent in just one decade. Clearly, the balanced budget requirement has placed no constraints whatsoever on the spending inclinations of New York City politicians, for the ability to conduct deficit spending is simply a matter of redefining the terms of the budget. The financial problems facing New York City in 1975 were caused, for the most part, by deficit spending which was not effectively constrained by the constitution, and was not able to be financed by an ever-shrinking tax base caused by the migration of firms and taxpayers trying to escape the highest tax burdens in the country.

Yet another financial gimmick, practiced by both off- and on-budget agencies, which helped pave the road to financial disaster was the rollover of short-term debt. The debt instruments used were bond anticipation notes (BANS), revenue anticipation notes (RANS), tax anticipation notes (TANS), and budget notes. Budget notes were short-term notes issued not in anticipation of future long-term bond issues, federal or state subsidies, or tax revenues—as were the former three instruments—but in anticipation of "unexpected" expenditures creating an "unforeseen deficit." These debt instruments were used to evade the constitutional limits on long-term debt, were authorized by the state legislature, and were severely abused. For example, future tax revenues were greatly overestimated. As one example, the state comptroller once noted that $502 million in real estate taxes listed on the city's books as "receivable" on June 30, 1975, were overstated by about $408 million![25] The same practice characterized the issuance of RANS as well, which led to a process whereby RANS and TANS would be issued, the revenue would not be forthcoming, RANS and TANS were reissued or "rolled over" to pay off the original debt, and so on. BANS were also rolled over, but for a slightly different reason. It was persistently claimed that it would save the city money if lower-cost, short-term notes were rolled over until long-term interest rates fell, at which point long-term bonds would be issued and the proceeds would be used, in part, to pay off the short-term notes. Overall, the short-term debt of New York City skyrocketed from $250 million in 1965 to over $4.5 billion in 1975—a 1,700 percent increase in 10 years—and constituted about three-fourths of New York City's total debt. By early 1974 the national economy had entered a period of inflationary recession, or stagflation, with long-term interest rates rising along with inflation. The conversion of more and more BANS into long-term debt was delayed further and further, and the city found itself issuing $750 million in short-term debt *per month* just to pay its bills. The investment bankers in the financial markets were all too willing to go along with this extravaganza as long as municipal bond sales, and the associated commissions, were brisk, and they believed that state and federal subsidies could save the city from bankruptcy. But in June of 1975 the bubble burst. The financial markets had had enough—they no longer thought that the city could pay off its debts and no one—bankers, state politicians or federal politicians—was willing to lend the city any more money. And the rest is all history.

New York's "Big MAC" Attack

Following in the footsteps of the New York State government, New York City went bankrupt for one reason and for one reason only:

[25]Ibid, p. 327.

Constitutional limits on government borrowing and spending were subverted on a large scale. As mentioned in the last chapter, after concluding that the off-budget antics of the statewide OBEs were the cause of the state's default in 1975, the "panel of experts" reporting to Governor Hugh Carey recommended that the answer to the state's financial problems lies not in constraining spending to keep within the taxpayers' means but rather, quite naturally for the politician, the creation of even more OBEs, "unburdened by the past." And the city followed suit by refusing to cut spending. The city sought bailouts from the state and federal governments, and the state quickly complied by creating yet another state-level OBE, the Municipal Assistance Corporation (Big MAC) which was to issue an unprecedented volume of moral obligation bonds to be used to fund the city's short-term debt. Since Big MAC has no taxing power and no assets, this solution merely forces the taxpayers of New York State to foot the bill through annual state appropriations which are the "moral obligation" of state politicians. Big MAC was authorized to issue an enormous $10 billion in debt, of which $6.1 billion was outstanding by June 1980.[26] For the first six months of its existence, however, Big MAC was unable to sell enough bonds to carry out its rescue mission. Only after the federal government agreed to provide over a billion dollars in loan guarantees and other forms of support could Big MAC sell adequate amounts of bonds.

In the final assessment, New York City's "solution" to bankruptcy has been to shift the cost to the taxpayers of the state and of the nation generally, while continuing to run deficits ranging in the hundreds of millions of dollars.[27] Many a political entrepreneur has launched a career by manipulating the various off-budget mechanisms in New York, and the latest newcomer, investment banker Felix Rohatyn, director of the Municipal Assistance Corporation, made his way into *Newsweek* magazine as "Mr. Fixit"—"The man who orchestrated New York City's recovery from . . . bankruptcy."[28] Making the most politically of his $10 billion blank check forced upon the taxpayers of New York State, Rohatyn announced in *Newsweek* a plan to go national with his procedures to "save the nation's cities." Presumably, this would mean increasing government borrowing by hundreds of billions of dollars at

[26]Municipal Assistance Corporation for the City of New York, *1980 Annual Report*, p. 32.

[27]McClelland and Magdovitz report that a private auditing firm, the first one *ever* to audit the books of New York City, found a deficit of $712 million in 1978, although the "official" listing was that the city had a *surplus* of $32 million.

[28]"Mr. Fixit for the Cities," *Newsweek*, May 4, 1981, p. 24.

a time when private borrowing is being increasingly crowded out. What the *Newsweek* article failed to mention was that if the federal government ever decided to withdraw its loan guarantee, Mr. Fixit, Big MAC, New York City, and maybe even New York State itself would not go national, but would go broke. In any event, if Mr. Fixit were to attempt to go national with his ideas, he would soon find that they are old hat, for as discussed above, off-budget enterprises such as Big MAC already exist nationwide and account for about 75 percent of all state and local government security sales.

The Washington Public Power Supply System Story

A recent article in *Fortune* magazine has the eye-catching title, "A Nuclear Fiasco Shakes the Bond Market."[29] The fiasco is not a melt-down, but what the article calls the "squalor and fantastic waste" of the off-budget Washington Public Power Supply System (WPPSS), or "Whoops" for short. WPPSS is an organization of 23 publicly owned utilities (19 public utility districts and the cities of Ellensberg, Richland, Seattle, and Tacoma) which in 1957 joined together to form a "municipal corporation" of the State of Washington—a "joint operating agency" authorized by state law which serves as the supply arm for its members. The stated purpose of creating WPPSS was to form an agency which "had broad powers to construct, finance, operate and sell power from electric generating plants."[30] WPPSS is an OBE which has invested in many large-scale projects financed by issuing revenue bonds. The squalor and waste mentioned in the *Fortune* article have resulted in scrapping two partially completed nuclear power plants. This action has left Washington utility customers with $2.25 billion in debt outstanding, a debt that is estimated to increase to $7.2 billion by the year 2018 when all outstanding bonds for those plants are retired, even though the plants will not provide a single kilowatt of power in return.

WPPSS continues construction on their other nuclear power plants at an ever-increasing cost. The initial cost estimates for all five plants of $4.2 billion has been revised upward to over $24 billion, and no power is expected before 1984. Originally, 1977 was the target date for

[29]Peter W. Bernstein, "A Nuclear Fiasco Shakes the Bond Market," *Fortune*, February 22, 1982, pp. 100–115.

[30]Washington State Senate Energy and Utilities Committee, *WPPSS Inquiry* (Seattle: Senate Energy and Utilities Committee, January 12, 1981), p. 8. WPPSS decided that it would be able to produce more electricity than its members could use, so has offered shares in the system to over 100 public and investor-owned utilities in Idaho, Oregon, and Montana as well as Washington.

completion of all five plants. These construction costs are expected to at least quadruple electric bills in 10 years and to push the outstanding debt of some of the member utilities to 70 or 80 percent of the value of all property in their jurisdictions—several times the legal limits on voter-approved general obligation debt. With over $7 billion in debt outstanding, WPPSS is now the largest issuer of revenue bonds ever, and according to the chairman of the Energy and Utilities Committee of the Washington State Senate, "default on the system's $7.7 billion in outstanding debt is a very realistic possibility."[31] Dozens of irate taxpayer groups have sprung up in Washington in recent months, and many are demanding an end to the WPPSS organization as well as answers to the question, "How did we get into this mess?"

The answer lies in the fact that OBEs such as WPPSS are eminently unaccountable to the taxpayers—even more so, apparently, than general purpose units of government which are subject to more direct taxpayer scrutiny and whose "managers" must face reelection.[32] In the case of WPPSS, other factors come into play as well. The Pacific Northwest is known for, among other things, its abundance of relatively cheap hydrolectric power and consequently, low utility rates. But in the late 1960s, local and state politicians observed that the law of demand was indeed working—falling electricity rates were boosting demand by about seven percent per year, and WPPSS management decided that the existing capacity could not meet future demands, boldly assuming consumption would continue to rise at that rate. The "Supply System" decided to get into the business of building nuclear power plants. The Bonneville Power Administration, a federal agency which produces power from dams built throughout the Northwest and sells it to local governments and private utilities, played a major role in convincing local political decision-makers to go ahead with the project. Bonneville was initially created to develop hydroelectric power production during the Great Depression and has long since accomplished that task, having spent billions of dollars, and provides residents of the Northwest with the cheapest and most abundant supply of electric power in North America. Nevertheless, Bonneville decided in the late 1960s to expand its empire into the nuclear power field and sent formal "notices of insufficiency" to its major customers, warning

[31]As quoted in Victor Zonana, "Rebellion Breaks Out in Northwest Over Skyrocketing Electricity Rates," *Wall Street Journal*, March 19, 1982, sec. 2, p. 31.

[32]And, most certainly, OBEs such as WPPSS are generally less efficient than private firms which must pass the test of the marketplace, where inefficiency in punished by lower profits and cost reduction is rewarded.

116

them that they would not be able to meet their projected (by Bonneville) needs and would be forced to start "rationing" electricity. Various special interests were soon to rally around the cause of nuclear power in the Northwest. Local politicians, although now lamenting their decisions and blaming everyone except themselves and, possibly, OPEC, for their troubles were quite enthusiastic about WPPSS, for many of them were to become members of the WPPSS board of directors which would hand out billions of dollars in construction contracts. Construction firms and unions also supported (and still support) WPPSS for obvious reasons, as did the investment banking community which made millions of dollars by underwriting WPPSS bonds. As an example of how lucrative such projects can be for investment bankers, in the Fall of 1981 Merrill Lynch underwrote an additional $750 million in WPPSS bonds and earned a $22.5 million commission—the largest in the firm's history.[33] With the powerful support of these groups, WPPSS began construction on five nuclear power plants simultaneously, which lead to financial disaster in just a few short years.

The disregard for cost effectiveness which is characteristic of all publicly owned enterprises, especially OBEs, is exemplified by a statement made by a Supply System director, who explained that "whenever cash was low, we would just toddle down to Wall Street."[34] This should come as no surprise, for it is typical of what happens when responsibility for one's actions is divorced from the actions themselves. As long as Supply System directors could borrow to finance construction, could pass on the costs to *future* voter-ratepayers, and the financial markets are willing and able to buy their bonds, there is little incentive for cost consciousness. In a very thorough study of the causes of WPPSS' financial failures, the state's Senate Energy and Utilities Committee concluded that the major cause of WPPSS problems was "mismanagement."[35] A more accurate description might be, perhaps, not mismanagement but "political management." With political control of resources, decisions are made not necessarily on the basis of any efficiency or equity criteria, but on the amount of votes or campaign contributions which can be earned. Consequently, the WPPSS board, which has the final say on all construction decisions, spread the work around to as many contractors as possible, utilizing 45 to 65 general contractors per job site. In contrast, Commonwealth Edison, a low-cost

[33]Bernstein, p. 112.

[34]Ibid., p. 110.

[35]Washington State Senate Energy and Utilities Committee.

private producer of nuclear power plants generally uses about three general contractors.[36] The confusion over "who should do what" on various job sites has led to long delays and, consequently, inflated construction costs. Adding further to the mayhem at the construction sites is the fact that each contractor is required to have his own support staff and equipment. Consequently, each construction site is littered with 40–50 cranes. By contrast, at other nuclear plant sites nine or 10 cranes are usually sufficient. These, and other duplications of effort have confounded any possibilities for meeting production schedules.

Also mentioned in the Senate Energy and Utilities Committee report on bureaucratic bungling at WPPSS construction sites are the consequences of WPPSS' use of "fast-track" construction methods, similar to those adopted by New York's Urban Development Corporation. A major problem created by WPPSS's fast-tracking stems from the practice of awarding contracts and commencing production before architectural and engineering design work is completed. When necessary design changes are made, "change orders" are issued which require the renegotiation of contracts and increases the time and cost of construction. Since the recontracting is not subjected to competitive bidding, many renewed contracts have increased costs by as much as 1,200 percent and delayed construction by as long as five years.[37] Even the architect-engineers hired to design the plants have delayed their work, not being held accountable to the terms of their contracts by WPPSS management, and have increased their fees several-fold in doing so. Among the engineering firms getting more money for less, or slower, service are Burns and Roe, which increased its fees from $29 million to $220 million; United Engineers, which went from $121 million to $358 million; and EBASCO, which upped its fee from $137 million to $430 million.[38] After gathering reams of evidence such as this, the state Senate Environment and Utilities Committee concluded:

> . . . management deficiency had a significant impact on costs and schedules. The cumulative impact of these problems leads the committee to conclude that WPPSS mismanagement has been the most significant cause of cost overruns and schedule delays on WPPSS projects.[39]

The concept of WPPSS cost overruns is a slippery one, however, for

[36]Ibid., p. 26.
[37]Ibid., p. 30.
[38]Ibid., p. 29.
[39]Ibid., p. 25.

118

WPPSS budgets are not really budgets, in the sense that they list an amount of money allocated to accomplish particular tasks, but are merely estimates of expected total costs to complete the projects. Thus, the only budget constraints faced by WPPSS management were the willingness of eager investment bankers to underwrite their bonds and of institutional investors to buy them. These constraints created very little incentive to contain costs and cost estimates rose from the original $4.2 billion to the current $24 billion. The end is nowhere in sight.

Disposing of Nuclear Waste

The extraordinary cost increases experienced by WPPSS which have angered the region's ratepayers led the System's board to vote in January 1981 to scrap two of the System's partially completed plants at an estimated cost of over $530 million, after selling $2.25 billion in bonds to build the plants. Estimated costs of completing the plants then stood at over $12 billion. Stories of cost overruns, the carnival-like atmosphere at construction sites, and future utility bills have infuriated ratepayers who have organized, marched, packed legislative hearings, and refused to pay their bills. In the November 4, 1981, elections irate taxpayer groups placed on the ballot an initiative that would require voter approval of WPPSS bond issues after July 1982. The initiative passed by a 59 percent to 41 percent margin despite the well-financed campaign against it led by contractors and investment bankers and warnings by such figures as the System's managing director, Robert Ferguson, that "any future vote that endangers financing for all five plants could have truly catastrophic consequences for the entire Pacific Northwest region."[40] Other board members have warned that ratepayers "would be visiting economic chaos on their communities by removing their obligations. The region's credit rating would be irreparably damaged, hurting local governments' ability to borrow money for schools, roads and sewers."[41] Despite these scare tactics (What could be worse for a city's credit rating than being affiliated with WPPSS?), the voters have remained adamant in their insistence upon placing WPPSS on-budget and subjecting its borrowings to voter approval, much to the dislike of investment bankers, contractors, unions, and the federal government who are all challenging the initiative in court. Three banks which are trustees of the bond funds—Seattle First National Bank, Morgan Guaranty Trust Co.

[40]Zonana, "Power System in Washington Dealt Setback," *Wall Street Journal,* November 5, 1981, p. 4.
[41]Zonana, "Rebellion Breaks Out," p. 31.

119

of New York, and Continental Illinois National Bank and Trust Co.—are pursuing litigation, and the initiative has been challenged by the U.S. Justice Department at the request of the federal Department of Energy.[42] To get the local utilities to go along with the original plan to build the nuclear plants, the Bonneville Power Administration agreed to assume part of the burden of paying off the bonds if the plants exceeded their target completion dates. Now that the plants have exceeded these dates, Bonneville is stuck with the tab, and has passed on the costs to *all* its ratepayers, increasing rates by 88 percent in 1980 and by 50 percent more in 1981.[43] Thus, Bonneville administrators have gotten their neighbors in the Justice Department to try to get them off the hook by claiming that the initiative requiring voter approval of bond issues "violates both federal and state constitutions." The Department of Justice claims that the initiative "interferes with Congressional policy regarding establishment of a reliable, stable power system in the Pacific Northwest and must give way to federal authority." Referring to WPPSS as "reliable" and "stable" certainly requires stretching the wildest of imaginations, but if the courts treat this case as they have treated similar cases in the past, i.e., justifying New York's moral obligation bonds, the initiative may be held illegal. A District Court judge has, in fact, ruled it to be unconstitutional, although that decision is being appealed. In the meantime, WPPSS continued to borrow at very high interest rates (as high as 18 percent, a truly remarkable rate for a tax-free obligation). Even though one would be hard-pressed to find a more haphazard operation than WPPSS, its bonds are still highly rated, at "triple-A." As one student of the municipal bond market has remarked, "The bond market, unlike corporations, has never been able to assess the underlying risk of such an enterprise. Somehow they believe that governments will always bail them out."[44] In this case, the bond market is correct, for Bonneville is in fact bailing out the System at the expense of *all* its customers, but is becoming increasingly reluctant to do so.

[42]"U.S. Sues Washington State for Requiring Voter Approval to Finance Nuclear Plants," *Wall Street Journal*, April 12, 1982.

[43]The Northwest Regional Power Act, adopted by Congress in 1980, gets Bonneville off the hook for the two scrapped plants by stating that Bonneville is to acquire responsibility for the plants only if they are "shown to be cost effective, and offer the alternatives of conservation, renewable resources, and co-generation, in that order, are exhausted and additional power is still needed." See L. Wayne, "Utility Setbacks on the Coast," *New York Times*, November 3, 1981, p. 31.

[44]Quotation of Annmarie Walsh, as cited in Wayne, p. 30.

The effects of WPPSS on ratepayers in the Northwest have been disastrous. In less than a decade they have gone from being "drunk with power" with the most abundant and least costly power in the nation, to the verge of defaulting on nearly $8 billion in outstanding debt, which to date has not yielded a single kilowatt of electricity. There is much concern that similar catastrophes may crop up elsewhere, for there are a number of large "joint-action" agencies similar to WPPSS throughout the country which are in the process of accumulating billions of dollars in debt. Table 22 lists the seven largest joint-action OBEs in the United States as of May 1981 along with their outstanding debt and planned expenditures.

Summary

In response to constitutional and statutory constraints on spending and borrowing, local governments in the United States have created thousands of OBEs which account for approximately three-fourths of all municipal security sales and are estimated to spend at least $35 to

Table 22

LARGEST JOINT-ACTION OBEs IN THE U.S., 1981
(millions of dollars)

Agency	Debt Outstanding as of May 31, 1981	Planned Future Expenditures
WPPSS	6,095	16,000
Municipal Electric Authority of Georgia	1,075	1,178
Texas Municipal Power Agency	850	230
North Carolina Municipal Power Agency No. 1	775	790
Massachusetts Municipal Wholesale Electric Co.	773	1,151
Intermountain Power Agency (Utah)	600	8,119
Platte River Power Authority (Colorado)	332	1,062

SOURCE: V. Zonana, "Dispute Flares on Financing Joint Agencies," *Wall Street Journal*, October 13, 1981, p. 35.

$50 billion annually. Off-budget mechanisms at the local level of gov-
ernment have greatly confounded attempts by taxpayers to cut taxes
and spending during the 1970s. Billions of dollars of spending and
borrowing have been placed off-budget in response to the taxpayer
rebellion in the 1970s, which leads to the conclusion that the growth
of local public spending may not have been impaired much at all by
the dozens of spending limitations enacted, but has merely been concealed. A recent study by the Tax Foundation[45] corroborates this, reporting
that state and local government *non-tax* revenues, mainly comprised of
the user fees of OBEs, rose about 1.5 times as fast as tax revenues
during the 1970s, increasing by 243 percent during that decade. The
Foundation finds that non-tax revenues topped property tax collections
in 1980 for the first time in history—contributing $75.8 billion in revenue
compared to $70 billion in property tax contributions.

In light of this evidence one can only conclude that the local public
sector, generally regarded by many as the most responsive to citizen-
taxpayers, is largely out of control and beyond the direct scrutiny of
taxpayers. Examples of how this extreme separation of ownership from
control in government can lead to undesirable outcomes are found in
the examples of the New York City bankruptcy of 1975, in which OBEs
played a major role, and the Washington Public Power Supply System,
which has become the largest participant ever in the municipal bond
market and is sitting precariously close to the brink of bankruptcy,
continually increasing the utility rates to its customers and not providing a single kilowatt of electricity. As seen in these two examples, the
implications for the local public economy of the operations of OBEs are
both profound and, at times, subtle. The next chapter examines the
activities of a particular type of OBE which operates at both the state
and local levels of government, the industrial development agency,
which is the fastest growing of all the types of OBEs in the United
States.

[45]Tax Foundation, *Monthly Tax Features*, May 1982.

VI. The Political Economy of Corporate Welfare: Industrial Revenue Bonds

Off-Budget Industrial Development

The fastest-growing type of off-budget operation at the state and local levels of government is the industrial development agency (IDA). Since the mid-1930s, state and local IDAs have issued tax-exempt industrial revenue bonds (IRBs) to finance the facilities of selected business enterprises. The original argument for the creation of IDAs has remained the same: Private capital markets allegedly fail to provide adequate financial resources to many firms, especially small businesses, and this reduces the economy's productive capacity and exacerbates unemployment. Each state and nearly every major city now has an IDA. Although it is impossible to gauge accurately the total volume of IRB sales, since many are privately negotiated with single banks, the Congressional Budget Office estimated total sales to exceed $10 billion in 1981, a 670 percent increase over the $1.3 billion in estimated sales in 1975.

A comparison of the rhetoric and reality of industrial development agencies demonstrates that they are more likely to reduce the economy's productive capacity rather than enhance it, that they distort the market process which normally allocates resources to their most productive uses, and that they provide an off-budget mechanism through which government planning replaces the plans of private individuals and firms.

The Development of IRB Finance

State and local governments issue two types of debt: general obligation bonds, which are backed by "the full faith and credit" of the issuing government and serviced with tax revenues; and revenue bonds, which are not guaranteed and are serviced by user charges from projects to be financed and from intergovernmental grants. During the late 19th century profligate general obligation borrowing practices by state and local governments led to frequent defaults and financial crises. Consequently, state statutory and constitutional restrictions on local government debt were imposed which placed limits on the amount of general obligation indebtedness as a percentage of the tax base, required referenda for bond issuance, restricted debt maturity dates (usually 20 years), and established interest rate ceilings.

To circumvent these restrictions, revenue bonds were adopted by local and state governments. Revenue bonds are generally issued by various public enterprises, the borrowing, spending, and employment of which are not included in the budget of the jurisdiction which created the "off-budget enterprise" (OBE). One of the first OBEs was the Port Authority of New York and New Jersey which was modeled after the Port of London Authority. These are now over 10,000 OBEs at the local level of government in the United States and thousands more at the state level.

In 1936 Mississippi became the first state to permit local governments to create a particular type of OBE, the industrial development agency (IDA), for issuing tax-exempt industrial revenue bonds to finance private businesses. In contrast to "industrial development bonds," which may be backed by the "full faith and credit" of the issuing government and are therefore on-budget and voter approved (although used much less frequently than IRBs), the only backing for IRBs is the credit of the borrowing firm, the revenue from projects financed and operated by the firm, or the firm's facilities. If the borrower defaults, the bondholder bears the loss. Since interest income from IRBs is tax exempt, private businesses can borrow at below-market interest rates.

By 1960, 17 states permitted the use of IRBs. Twenty-five additional states passed IRB-enabling legislation during the 1960s, and the volume of reported IRB sales rose by 1,700 percent between 1960 and 1968, from $100 million to $1.8 billion.[1] In 1968, IRBs constituted approximately nine percent of long-term, tax-exempt municipal security sales compared with just one percent in 1960. This increase was due largely to the rise in issue size, which grew from an average of $360,000 in 1957 to $7.8 million in 1967. Large corporations had come to realize the usefulness of IRBs in financing investment projects. For example, between 1962 and 1968 all major tire manufacturers (Armstrong, Cooper, Dunlop, Firestone, Goodrich, Goodyear, Mansfield, Mohawk, Uniroyal) used IRB financing, as did many other large manufacturers.[2] Critics of IRB financing soon began to levy charges against these companies: They used "public funds" to subsidize projects that would have been

[1]Congressional Budget Office, *Small Issue Industrial Revenue Bonds* (Washington, D.C.: CBO, April 1981), p. 9.
[2]Ibid.

124

undertaken without subsidies; the projects resulted in revenue losses to the treasury; and they led to an increase in state and local borrowing costs. The Congress was sympathetic to these views and in 1968 passed the Revenue Expenditure and Control Act which intended to limit IRB use. The act withdrew the tax exemption for all but a number of exceptions such as air and water pollution control equipment, airports, docks, wharves, electricity, gas and water services, industrial parks, parking, mass transportation, housing, sewage, sports facilities, and trade shows and convention centers. The act also exempted bonds with a face value not exceeding $5 million to finance plants and equipment for industrial facilities. The purpose of this exemption was to change the focus of IRB finance so as "to assist *small* businesses in locating in a community"[3] (emphasis added).

In 1978 President Carter, anxious to expand the Urban Development Action Grant (UDAG) program, proposed that the limits for "small-issue IRBs," often used in combination with UDAG grants, be raised to $10 million. Congress complied and the higher limit went into effect on January 1, 1979.

Measuring the current volume of IRB sales is virtually impossible, since most IRBs are small issues which are negotiated with local banks and need not be reported to the Securities and Exchange Commission. Nevertheless, some estimates have been made, and the most reliable are probably those of the Congressional Budget Office which surveyed IRB-issuing agencies in each state.[4] These estimates are shown in Table 23 and remain underestimates since some states do not maintain records of IRB sales. Even with these data limitations it is clear that IRB sales have grown dramatically, having increased by 546 percent between 1975 and 1980.

The Industrial Development Agency

The conduit through which IRBs are issued is the industrial development agency, which exists at both the state and local levels of government. Each state has established at least one IDA at the state level of government. In recent years the activities of IDAs have expanded substantially, as is evidenced by the rapid increase in IRB sales and the fact that total agency budgets increased by over 300 percent during the 1966–73 period, from $2.57-7.63 million.[5]

[3]Wilbur D. Mills, *Congressional Record*-House, October 10, 1968, p. 30603.

[4]Congressional Budget Office, *Small Issue Bonds*.

[5]Institute of International Law and Economic Development, *The Industrial Revenue Bond As a Financial Attraction Device* (Washington, D.C.: Economic Development Administration, 1978), p. 144.

Table 23

ESTIMATES OF THE VOLUME OF SMALL ISSUE INDUSTRIAL
REVENUE BONDS, 1975–1980
(billions of dollars)

Year	Congressional Budget Office	Public Securities Association	Daily Bond Buyer
1975	1.3	0.5	0.5
1976	1.5	0.4	0.3
1977	2.3	0.8	0.5
1978	3.5	0.9	0.6
1979	7.1	1.7	1.3
1980	8.4	1.6	1.4

SOURCE: Congressional Budget Office, *Small Issue Industrial Revenue Bonds* (Washington, D.C.: CBO, April 1981), p. 14.

At the local level of government IDAs are established by local governments and managed by governing bodies comprised of at least five political appointees who are usually local politicians or professional "urban planners." A key role is played in IRB financing of private businesses by "local industrial development corporations" (LIDCs). LIDCs are "non-profit" corporations formed by local business interests. Their purpose and role in the IRB-financing process has been succinctly stated by the Council of State Governments:

> Many . . . industrial finance authorities do not make loans directly to industrial prospects. In these states the LIDC serves as a bridge between the authority and the new industry. In some states this procedure is necessitated by constitutional provisions prohibiting the loan of public monies to private industry. The LIDC, as a non-profit corporation, however, can hold title to industrial property and receive the loan.[6]

The Rhetoric and Reality of Industrial Development Finance

Although many states outlaw the practice of tax exemptions for selected private firms or individuals, IRBs have always survived these limits because of LIDCs as well as what is known as the "public service doctrine."[7] This "doctrine" states that projects financed by IRBs must confer a "public benefit," such as the development of a new industry

[6]Council of State Governments, *Economic Development in the States* (Chicago Council of State Governments, 1966), p. 1.

[7]Institute of International Law and Economic Development, "The Industrial Revenue Bond," p. 76.

or a reduction in unemployment. A typical example is the Pennsylvania Industrial and Commercial Development Authority Law, which states that local industrial development authorities shall operate:

> for the purposes of alleviating unemployment, maintaining employment at a high level . . . and developing business opportunities by the construction, improvement, rehabilitation, revitalization, and financing of industrial, commercial, manufacturing, research and development enterprises.[8]

These activities are said to "promote the health, safety, morals, and general welfare of the people."

The rationale for government intervention through IRB financing is therefore based on the classic notion of market failure. That is, it is alleged that if for some reason information about market opportunities, production technology, access to capital markets, etc., is not available to all producers, market forces will not allocate resources in an efficient way and the economy will produce below its capacity. The market failure argument has been used in defense of IRB finance of "small" businesses in particular, given the emphasis which has been placed on limiting industrial revenue bond use to "small issues."

Even though "market failure" is the principal rationale for public policy intervention, it is now widely acknowledged that the "inadequacy of market outcomes" is only a necessary, not a sufficient, condition for government intervention in the economy.[9] Public policy formulation requires that market failures be compared to the prospective failures of government intervention actually exacerbating problems caused by "market inadequacies," i.e., urban renewal and poverty programs, regulation of the airline and trucking industries, and so on. When political resource allocation replaces market allocation, the consequences are likely to be arbitrary and are often contrary to the interests of the general public. Consumer sovereignty, which induces producers to allocate resources to their most highly valued use, is replaced by "political sovereignty." And past experience provides no reason to expect politicians to be particularly concerned with allocative efficiency. Equity, however defined, is no more likely under political resource allocation than market allocation, and politics can create greater ineq-

---

[8]Ibid.

[9]See Charles Wolf, Jr., "A Theory of Nonmarket Failure: Framework for Implementation Analysis," *Journal of Law and Economics*, April 1979, pp. 107–139.

uities than does the market.[10] How politicians allocate resources that are under their control will depend upon their perceptions of the personal benefits (votes, campaign contributions, etc.) that accrue from alternative allocations. As James Buchanan has observed:

> Politicians are politicians because they want to be. They are no more robots than other men. Yet the politician who would do nothing other than reflect the preferences of his constituents would, in fact, be robotlike in his behavior. Few, if any, politicians are so restricted. They seek office because they seek "profit," in the form of "political income," which will normally be obtained only if their behavior is not fully in accord with the desires of electoral majorities. Those men who are attracted to politics as a profession are likely to be precisely those who have considerable interest in promoting their own version of good government, along with those who see the opportunities for direct and indirect bribes, and those who evaluate political office as a means toward other ends.[11]

Thus, even if there are market imperfections which preclude "small" firms from competing, whether industrial development agencies can promote economic growth and reduce unemployment is uncertain. Such goals will only be pursued if it is in the interest of political decision-makers to do so. In fact, it may be contrary to the interests of IDA managers to reduce unemployment and to increase economic growth. With low unemployment and steady growth, there is little need for an "agency" to "promote" low unemployment, just as without an "energy crisis" there is little need for a Department of Energy.

The Effects of IRB Finance

Can IDAs be expected to improve the allocation of resources caused by market imperfections and to aid the economy in producing at full capacity? At the outset, it is important to recognize that in one very important respect IDAs intensify rather than ameliorate market imperfections. Namely, when IDAs grant preferential treatment to failing businesses, as they often do, consumers are forced to pay (through taxes) for goods and services they would not otherwise prefer, and

[10]A classic example is federal "urban renewal" programs which have demolished about twice as many housing units as they have replaced, and a large percentage of those replaced have been for middle- and upper-income individuals. Wealthier people are not only better off competing in the marketplace than less wealthy people, but are also more influential politically.

[11]James M. Buchanan, "Why Does Government Grow?" in Thomas E. Borcherding, ed., *Budgets and Bureaucrats: The Sources of Government Growth* (Durham, N.C.: Duke University Press, 1977), pp. 3–18.

inefficient producers make use of resources that would otherwise be put to more highly valued uses in other industries. Both consumer sovereignty and production efficiency are reduced. Conferring preferential tax status on failing businesses, "large" or "small," constitutes nothing more than special interest legislation which distorts the structure of the market from that which would otherwise emerge.

Once IDAs are established and begin to prop up failing businesses, there are strong incentives for their continued growth and expansion. The reason for this is that the selected tax exemptions are provided to relatively small, concentrated groups, whereas the costs (in resources diverted from their highest-valued uses) are widely dispersed among the general public and are well hidden. The selected group obviously has a strong incentive to promote the expanded use of IRB finance, while the average taxpayer has little incentive to oppose it, even though the *total* costs to society may far exceed the benefits to the firms.

Can IDAs be expected to aid "small" businesses which would otherwise be precluded from operating due to market imperfections? There is no doubt that many small businesses, failing or otherwise, receive IRB financing from local IDAs. It is also quite clear that there is a great deal of "political income" to be earned by offering IRB financing to large as well as small firms. In fact the record clearly shows that IRBs have been used to finance large manufacturing firms as well as auto dealerships, motels, doctors' and lawyers' offices, cable TV systems, banks, ski resorts, bowling alleys, country clubs, topless bars, and "adult" bookstores.[12] Thus, a large volume of IRBs are used to finance the nation's largest corporations. Ironically, the subsequent advantages granted to larger corporations allow them to drive smaller retailers and merchants out of business in many cities.

The Congressional Budget Office recently completed a study of IRBs and found that about 16 percent of the total volume of small issue IRBs in 1978 and 1979 went to the top 50 companies on the Fortune 500 list. Table 24 lists selected Fortune 500 (industrial and nonindustrial) firms which received $1.2 billion in IRB financing in 1978 and 1979. Other

[12]Robert M. Bleiberg, "Corporate Food Stamps," *Barron's*, August 17, 1981, p. 7. As an example of the virtually indiscriminate use of IRBs by local politicians, when rumors that the Reagan administration was considering the curtailment of IRBs, politicians in Baltimore, Maryland, held two days of "marathon meetings" in which they approved 81 bond authorizations worth $715 million—three times what the city approved in all of 1980. Many of the newly issued IRBs listed no specific project, and $350 million in bonds identify no developer, bank, or project, but were simply put in for future use, in case IRBs are eliminated. See M. Shapiro, "Maryland Counties Scramble for Tax-Exempt Bonds," *Washington Post*, October 17, 1981. p. A-1.

Table 24
SELECTED FORTUNE 500 FIRMS RECEIVING IRB FINANCING IN 1978–79

Firm	Amount of Bond Issue
Procter & Gamble Co.	$ 6,500,000
General Mills, Inc.	26,200,000
K-Mart Corp.	90,140,000
Exxon Corp.	24,000,000
Mobil Oil Corp.	63,000,000
Standard Oil Co. of Ohio	675,000,000
Phillips Petroleum	20,000,000
Atlantic Richfield Co.	61,055,000
Union Oil of California	22,500,000
Burlington Industries	9,500,000
Mead Corp.	7,800,000
Ford Motor Co.	23,345,000
McDonald's Corp.	17,400,000
Hoover Universal, Inc.	20,000,000
B. F. Goodrich Co.	3,000,000
Goodyear Tire & Rubber Co.	20,890,000
Weyerhaeuser Co.	18,000,000
Norton Co.	28,800,000 ·
Dana Corp.	13,605,000
Union Camp Corp.	20,470,000
Georgia Pacific Corp.	9,500,000
Joy Manufacturing Co.	7,200,000

SOURCE: *Moody's Municipal and Government Manual* (New York: Dun and Bradstreet Co., 1981).

Fortune 500 manufacturing firms received an additional $390 million. As shown in Table 24, large manufacturing and retailing firms have used IRBs to finance major investment projects. For example, K-Mart financed 96 stores in 19 states between 1975 and 1980, including 35 stores in 1980 alone. Similarly, McDonald's financed 32 new restaurants in Pennsylvania and Ohio in 1979.[13] Other major companies making use of IRBs include Nabisco, PepsiCo, Allied Chemical, Container Corporation of America, and International Paper, to name only a few.

[13]*Moody's Bond Record*, January 1981, pp. 109–22.

Overall, more than half of the Fortune 500 firms received IRB financing during the 1978-79 period.

Thus, IRBs further distort the efficient (market) allocation of resources by providing "tax exemptions" to selected firms, large and small. Not applying laws regarding tax reduction equally to *all* firms and individuals is sure to disrupt the entrepreneurial process whereby scarce resources tend to be allocated to their most highly valued uses. Since market prices are altered by such arrangements, information regarding true benefits and costs is distorted, which makes it difficult, if not impossible, to discover the most highly valued resource use or least-cost production techniques.

IRB finance of large corporate enterprises imposes further costs on society by establishing regional monopolies in various industries. One can readily think of how the construction of a K-Mart can drive small local retailers who have not benefited from IRBs out of business. Established merchants and restauranteurs in many cities have protested IRB financing of their larger competitors but have had limited success in restraining their use. In July 1980, however, over 2,200 voters in Ravalli County, Montana, signed petitions calling for a referendum on the use of $4 million in IRBs to construct a K-Mart shopping center. Local merchants eventually succeeded in having the bond issue placed on the November election ballot. The bond issue was defeated.[14]

This particular type of "political warfare" amplifies yet another cost of government intervention by IDAs which tends to reduce the economy's productive capacity. Namely, the existence of a mechanism for distributing IRBs creates "economic rents" or above-normal profits. Consequently, resources will be used in obtaining, maintaining, extending, and (by some) eliminating these rents. The use of resources for purposes of "rent seeking" (and "rent avoidance") represents a deadweight loss to society since these resources are used in attempts to transfer wealth rather than to produce additional goods and services.[15] The establishment of industrial development agencies will therefore reduce the economy's productive capacity, but provides a means by which local politicians can capture rewards (political profit) from handing out government empowerments. For example, in 1980 the village of South Barrington, Illinois, sold $18 million worth of IRBs

[14]Congressional Budget Office, *Small Issue Bonds*, p. 30.

[15]For a discussion of rent seeking, see James Buchanan, Robert Tollison, and Gordon Tullock, eds., *Toward A Theory of the Rent-Seeking Society* (College Station: Texas A&M Press, 1980).

to finance two Marshall Field department stores and a Carson, Pirie, Scott department store. For its efforts the local IDA managers collected "fees" of $100,000 from Marshall Field and $67,000 from Carson, Pirie, Scott.[16]

The lobbying costs of IRB beneficiaries are only a part of the total costs associated with rent seeking. Total rent-seeking costs would include those borne by firms which lobbied unsuccessfully for subsidies as well as those borne by investment bankers and law firms which also benefit from increased IRB sales, and by those businesses, i.e., smaller merchants,, who oppose IRB financing. For example, the first vice-president of a major investment banking firm has boasted that "we've been responsible for changing the laws (regarding enabling legislation for IRB sales) in fifteen states."[17]

There are, of course, benefits to IRB finance inasmuch as IRBs provide a form of tax relief, albeit indirect. However, it is unlikely that the net benefits of IRB finance would be positive, given the costly economic distortions discussed above. Ideally, the free access of all firms to IRB finance would be more conducive to stimulating production and employment while limiting various economic distortions. Such an alternative would be analogous to across-the-board reductions in the taxation of corporate income, but is not likely to materialize.

Summary and Conclusions

In sum, industrial revenue bonds tend to distort, rather than facilitate, the market process. Both consumer sovereignty and production efficiency are compromised when IRBs are used to support failing or inefficient business enterprises. Further, the increasing use of IRB finance alters relative prices, which makes it more costly for consumers and producers to make accurate decisions regarding resource uses. The entrepreneurial process whereby resources are put to their most highly valued uses is disrupted. In essence, IRB finance substitutes political resource allocation for the market allocation of resources, and the results are neither efficient nor equitable. The economy's productive capacity is reduced when IRBs are used to selectively help some firms through special tax exemptions chosen by political rather than economic criteria, and when resources are used to obtain such exemptions rather than to produce additional goods and services.

[16]*Chicago Tribune*, May 11, 1980.

[17]Annmarie Walsh, *The Public's Business* (Cambridge: MIT Press, 1980), p. 151.

While it is indeed desirable to reduce the burden of corporate taxation and regulation, there are surely more direct ways of doing so rather than the selective distribution of industrial revenue bonds.

VII. The Underground Federal Government

Budget Reform and the Form of the Budget

In keeping with the traditions established at the state and local levels of government, the federal government has responded to recent taxpayer demands for fiscal restraint by marshalling hundreds of billions of dollars in spending off-budget via the credit markets. There are three basic ways in which, through the credit markets, federal spending is hidden and kept off the budget. First, numerous agencies have simply been deleted from the budget. Second, government control over resource allocation is extended by guaranteeing loans made to specially privileged individuals, businesses, and governments. Third, there are numerous privately owned, but federally sponsored and controlled, enterprises such as the Federal National Mortgage Association, which are also off-the-books borrowers.

In addition to manipulating credit market activities, federal politicians have increasingly recognized that, in principle, anything that can be accomplished through taxing and spending can also be accomplished by regulation. All of these activities must be taken into account to assess accurately the role of the federal government in the economy.

The Congressional Budget and Impoundment Control Act of 1974 has been praised by *U.S. News & World Report* as a "revolutionary budget reform intended to give Congress a tighter grip on the nation's purse strings."[1] The Budget Act emerged from a recognition that existing budgetary procedures generated a bias toward overspending and budget deficits. Prior to 1974, the total amount of federal spending was the product of many individual appropriations decisions; no explicit limit was ever placed on the total amount of public expenditure. Each congressman had then, as he does now, a very strong incentive to maximize spending on his own voting constituency, while limiting the extent to which they must pay for the spending. But no congressman was required to take responsibility for the total amount of federal

---

[1]As quoted in James M. Buchanan and Richard E. Wagner, *Democracy in Deficit: The Political Legacy of Lord Keynes* (New York: Academic Press, 1977), p. 156.

spending that resulted from the appropriations process. The Budget Reform Act created a budget committee for each house responsible for setting overall targets for revenues, expenditures, and the resultant deficit (or surplus). The Congressional Budget Office was created to assist in this process.

The main impact of the Budget Act is to make taxing, spending, and deficit levels explicit and to hold Congress accountable for them; the law itself does nothing to curb spending. The relatively mild budgetary discipline set forth in the Budget Act elicited a great deal of "back-door spending" at the federal level. In the wake of the Budget Act, numerous agencies have been placed off-budget and beyond the purview of any appropriations process. Thus, while the Congress was publicly proclaiming a need for fiscal discipline in federal budget matters and enacting legislation to deal with the problem of "uncontrollable" spending, it was simultaneously establishing mechanisms through which spending could be placed off-budget. Off-budget federal outlays, by agency, since 1973 are shown in Table 25. Although the estimated $23.2 billion in off-budget outlays in 1981 was only about 5 percent of the federal budget, this amount has increased by an astounding 23,100 percent since 1973. Most recently, the Synthetic Fuels Corporation, which began operations in 1981, was also placed off-budget. Congress had previously authorized $20 billion for the development of this industry. The penchant for back-door federal spending is obviously nonpartisan. Both the Democratic-controlled House and the Republican-controlled Senate, at the insistence of the Reagan administration, voted to place the Strategic Petroleum Reserve "off the books." There have even been bipartisan proposals for dealing with the Social Security crisis by placing the Social Security program, with over $220 billion in expenditures in 1982, off-budget!

As is evident from Table 25 the Federal Financing Bank (FFB) is by far the most active off-budget agency.[2] The FFB, a part of the Treasury Department, does business with both on- and off-budget agencies. The predominant activity of the FFB is the purchase of agency debt from funds obtained by borrowing directly from the Treasury. FFB borrowing is not, however, included as part of the Treasury's budget outlays; interest payments from the FFB to the Treasury are, nevertheless, counted as *deductions* from Treasury outlays. Consequently, FFB bor-

[2]For background information on the FFB, see Congressional Budget Office, *Loan Guarantees: Current Concerns and Alternatives for Control*, (Washington, D.C.: U.S. Government Printing Office, 1979).

Table 25

OFF-BUDGET OUTLAYS BY AGENCY
(billions of dollars)

	1973	1974	1975	1976	TQ	1977	1978	1979	1980	1981ᵉ
Federal Financing Bank (1974)	—	.1	6.4	5.9	2.6	8.2	10.6	13.2	14.5	23.1
Rural Electrification and Telephone Revolving Fund (1973)	.1	.5	.5	.2	.1	.4	.1	—	—	—
Rural Telephone Bank (1973)	*	.1	.1	.1	*	.1	.1	.1	.2	.2
Pension Benefit Guaranty Corporation (1974)	—	—	*	*	*	*	*	*	—	—
United States Postal Service Fund (1974)	—	.8	1.1	1.1	.7	.2	.5	.9	.4	.2
United States Railway Association (1973)	—	*	*	.1	*	.2	.1	.1	*	-.3
Total Off-Budget Outlays	0.1	1.4	8.1	7.3	3.4	8.7	10.3	12.4	14.3	23.2

ᵉestimate—Office of Management and Budget estimate in fiscal 1982 budget document
*less than $50 million
SOURCE: Office of Management and Budget, *Budget of the United States Government*, 1982.

137

rowing actually results in a reduction in outlays reported by the Treasury Department. In essence, the FFB serves as an intermediary which permits the spending of federal agencies to be placed off-budget.

A second type of FFB activity is the purchase of agency loans or loan assets. When a federal agency sells a loan to a private entity, the loan is considered repaid for budgetary purposes. Loans made by federal agencies are afforded the same treatment when the FFB is the purchaser. Proceeds from the sale are counted as loan repayments rather than as a means of financing and thus are an offset to the agency's gross expenditures. An agency's on-budget loan can therefore be converted to an off-budget loan by selling it to the FFB. In 1981, about 90 percent of all federal agency loans and loan asset sales were sold to the FFB.

Rather than selling individual loans, an agency can sometimes pool its loans and issue securities backed by the pooled loans. These securities, known as "Certificates of Beneficial Ownership," are then turned over to the FFB for cash, placing them off-budget. The agency has cash to loan again, and can repeat the process as many times as it chooses. This procedure allows federal agencies to make loans to privileged customers with virtually no budgetary limit.

Another type of FFB activity is the granting of off-budget loans to guaranteed borrowers, usually when a federal agency sanctions a loan between a private lender and a private borrower. The result is an interest subsidy to the borrower at no *explicit* cost to the Treasury unless a borrower defaults. Frequently, however, an agency will ask the FFB to act as the private lender and purchase the borrower's note. In this case the loan guarantee becomes, in effect, a direct loan from the government which is not reflected in the budget. In 1981 FFB purchases of loan guarantees amounted to over $10 billion.

The outstanding holdings of the FFB in 1981, by type of activity, are shown in Table 26. As seen there, total outstanding holdings as of 1981 exceeded $107 billion. The primary beneficiaries have been the Farmers Home Administration (FmHA) and, to a lesser extent, many other agencies which can transfer enormous sums off-budget. The FmHA increased its loans by over 500 percent in the first five years after the establishment of the FFB.[3]

In sum, the activities of the FFB give federal politicians and bureaucrats a virtual blank check, with no *direct* budgetary consequences with

[3]Staff Report, Joint Economic Committee, U.S. Congress, *The Underground Federal Economy* (Washington, D.C.: U.S. Government Printing Office, April 20, 1982), p. 12.

Table 26
FFB OUTSTANDING HOLDINGS, 1981
(billions of dollars)

Activity	
Agency Debt	
Export-Import Bank	12.4
Tennessee Valley Authority	10.9
Other	1.6
Loan Assets*	
Farmers Home Administration	48.8
Rural Electrification Administration	2.6
Other	.4
Direct Loans to Guaranteed Borrowers	
REA loans to rural electric cooperatives	12.3
DOD loans for foreign military sales	9.1
Other	9.2
Total FFB Outstanding Holdings	107.3

*Primarily Certificates of Beneficial Ownership
SOURCE: Staff Report, Joint Economic Committee, U.S. Congress, *The Underground Federal Economy* (Washington, D.C.: U.S. Government Printing Office, April 20, 1982), p. 12.

which to dispense rapidly growing amounts of loans and subsidies to their constituent interest groups.[4] The political costs of federal largesse are effectively reduced by the FFB. As an indication of the political bonanza being enjoyed by various federal politicians and their supporting federal agencies, Table 27 lists outstanding FFB loans to guaranteed borrowers during the 1980–82 period. At a time of supposed fiscal restraint by members of Congress and the Reagan administration, FFB loans outstanding to guaranteed borrowers are expected to double in just two years, with one category, loans for low-rent housing, increasing by 340 percent.

In essence, the loan guarantees administered by the FFB constitute the "back-door financing" of additional government control and regulation of the economy's resources. Government agencies can grant special privileges to select groups of individuals, business firms, foreign governments, or even other government-sponsored enterprises (e.g.,

[4]There is no free lunch, of course. The economic effects of the FFB are discussed shortly.

139

Table 27

OUTSTANDING FFB LOANS TO GUARANTEED BORROWERS,
FISCAL YEARS 1980–82
(billions of dollars)

Agency and Borrower	1980	1981	1982ᵉ
REA guaranteed loans to rural electric cooperatives	8.4	12.3	16.5
DOD guaranteed loans for foreign military sales	7.2	9.1	11.1
HUD guaranteed loans to low-rent public housing	.1	.9	3.5
TVA guaranteed loans to Seven States Energy Corporation	.7	.9	1.2
Other	2.8	3.1	3.9
Total Loans Outstanding	21.5	30.6	41.5

ᵉestimates

SOURCE: *Underground Federal Economy*, p. 13.

the Tennessee Valley Authority), without being subjected to congressional scrutiny and, theoretically, without budgetary limit. The FFB, therefore, provides federal agencies an opportunity for wide-scale intrusion into credit market decision-making.

Economic Implications of FFB Loan Guarantees

Many advocates of free enterprise have objected to congressional action that granted New York City and the Chrysler Corporation several billion dollars in highly publicized loan guarantees. The New York City loan guarantee does little to address the city's fiscal problem—deficit spending—and encourages other cities to follow the same route to bankruptcy, with hopes of being rescued by the taxpaying public. The Chrysler loan guarantee, its critics observe, simply bails out an inefficient business enterprise by siphoning over a billion dollars in credit that would be put to more highly valued uses by more credit-worthy borrowers. The general consequences of subsidizing failing businesses are well-known and are diagnosed worldwide as the "British disease." Great Britain's anemic industrial performance of the past several decades is due largely to the fact that the British government forces taxpayers to subsidize on a wide scale failing or grossly inefficient business enterprises. The Chrysler loan guarantee is a step in this direction; it has been denounced both by conservatives, who favor free enterprise and oppose subsidies to business, and by liberals, who fear the powers of "big business." The Chrysler and New York City loans pale in comparison, however, with the off-budget guaranteed loans administered by the FFB. These two loan guarantees were subjected to congressional oversight and subsequently received much media exposure, but FFB loan guarantee decisions are made by a few nonelected bureaucrats in a small office located at the Department of Treasury.[5] This system provides opportunities for "social engineering" by nonelected bureaucrats that the Chrysler loan could not. This is evident from the $2 billion in off-budget loans recently extended by the FFB to the TVA.[6] In 1979 the TVA decided that its nuclear fuel inventory had become excessive due to nuclear power plant construction delays. To remove the burden of excessive inventories from its books, the TVA created a wholly owned subsidiary—the Seven States Energy Corporation—with which TVA could enter into a lease-back arrangement. Seven States would purchase TVA's nuclear fuel inventory, and then lease it back as needed. To finance the arrangement, TVA originally approached a private investment banking firm, which suggested a $1 billion line of credit. Before the agreement was completed, however, the Treasury Department suggested that the FFB could provide the credit and would increase the amount of the loan to $2 billion. Thus, the TVA, in effect, extended a $2 billion line of credit to itself—more than either the Chrysler or New York City loan guarantees—and Congress was not involved at all. This has far-reaching implications for the future role of the federal government in allocating credit—a role which has, in the past, been played with most unfortunate consequences in terms of both equity and efficiency. According to the FFB Act, *any* entity wholly owned by the federal government has this access to off-budget federal financing. Several such entities do exist and have the legal authority to order the FFB to lend money to anyone, provided that they guarantee the loan.[7]

[5]The authors attempted to contact FFB officials, but found that their agency is neither in the District of Columbia phone book nor in the current listings of federal agencies.

[6]TVA is a regional OBE, obtaining most of its revenue from the sale of revenue bonds. It does, however, receive federal aid in the form of appropriations, grants, and guaranteed loans. The following example is found in C. Hardin and A. Denzau, *The Unrestrained Growth of Federal Credit Programs* (St. Louis: Washington University Center for the Study of American Business, December 1981).

[7]There are at least 20 such agencies, including the Commodity Credit Corporation, the Export-Import Bank, Corporation for Public Broadcasting, Government National Mortgage Association, Community Development Corporation, U.S. Railway Association, Pension Benefit Guarantee Corporation, Legal Services Corporation, and others.

In addition to substituting inefficient and inequitable political resource allocation for the more efficient market allocation of capital, the existence of the FFB also *increases* the borrowing costs to the federal government, despite the argument that by pooling agency borrowing, financing costs are reduced. The reason for this is that the increased interest rate on federal debt resulting from FFB borrowing from the Treasury is far more expensive than the minimal savings to federal agencies. Agency debt appeals to a different market than does Treasury debt, as the difference in interest rates attests. When the Treasury issues more debt (to finance the FFB), it crowds the market segment to which its issues appeal, and that forces rates up on Treasury debt. This, one would think, invalidates the entire economic (but not the political) rationale for the FFB.[8]

Loan Guarantees and the Allocation of Credit

In addition to the loan guarantee and other functions of the FFB, there are over 150 federal loan guarantee programs administered by federal agencies, which comprise yet another category of off-budget operations. Loan guarantees to individuals, businesses, state and local governments, or foreign governments are only reflected in the budget if the borrower, dealing through a private bank, defaults. In that case, the federal government is liable for part or all of the principal and interest on the loan. Although not reflected in the budget document, loan guarantees serve the same purpose as direct, tax-financed appropriations: They provide transfer payments to select groups at the expense of the general public. The major difference, of course, between tax-financed subsidies and loan guarantees is that the latter are far less visible and do not arouse as much taxpayer resistance as would the former, in many instances. For example, a tax-financed subsidy to a college student whose parents earn $100,000 per year will surely meet more resistance, especially from the less wealthy, than will a guaranteed loan which is often (mistakenly) not considered to entail a subsidy. The partial or full guarantee of such loans does, however, permit the favored borrowers to borrow at reduced interest rates. Because of the hidden nature of these "interest subsidies" loan guarantees have become the largest component of federal credit activity, as shown in Table 28, which lists the growth of federal loan guarantees, as well as on- and

[8]This point was brought to our attention by Professor Yale Brozen of the University of Chicago in personal correspondence.

142

Table 28

ANNUAL FEDERAL CREDIT OUTLAYS, FISCAL YEARS 1974–1982
(billions of dollars)

| | Loan Category | | |
Year	Direct Loans, On-Budget	Direct Loans, Off-Budget	Guaranteed Loans
1974	12.3	3.5	31.8
1975	12.9	10.8	31.1
1976	18.8	10.2	31.8
1977	14.7	13.6	43.3
1978	23.5	16.4	45.5
1979	21.0	17.3	60.5
1980	25.7	23.6	68.7
1981ᵉ	24.6	32.2	90.5
1982ᵉ	28.1	26.2	101.5

ᵉestimates
SOURCE: *Budget of the U.S. Government, Special Analyses,* various years.

off-budget direct loans, from 1974 to 1982. The data indicate that loan guarantees are by far the largest component of federal credit activity, comprising over 65 percent of all credit activity and about four times the volume of direct, on-budget loans. They are also the fastest-growing type of federal credit activity, having increased by 320 percent since 1974.

The major costs of federal loan guarantee programs, like the benefits, are indirect. A major difference, however, is that the benefits of loan guarantees accrue to well-organized interest groups, whereas the costs are widely dispersed among the general public. The predominant indirect cost of federal loan guarantees is borne by less-favored borrowers who are crowded out of the credit market or who must pay higher interest rates on the loans that are obtained. Loan guarantees tend to increase the overall demand for credit while at the same time reducing the supply of credit available to nonguaranteed borrowers. The effect is to increase the rates charged to nonguaranteed borrowers to levels higher than they would otherwise be, which crowds out much private borrowing by businesses, individuals, and state and local governments. This process seriously distorts the market process whereby unregulated markets allocate credit to its most highly valued uses—enhancing economic growth.

143

Credit markets serve the role of evaluating the riskiness of alternative projects, and those with higher probabilities of failure (to meet consumer demands) are charged higher borrowing costs. In this way, the credit markets provide consumers and producers with invaluable information regarding the most productive uses of resources. Loan guarantees, by socializing risk, make it impossible for consumers and producers to make accurate benefit-cost calculations, and resources are put to lower-valued, not higher-valued, uses once politics rather than the market is used to allocate credit. At times when high interest rates force private firms to invest in only the most productive projects promising very high yields, federally assisted borrowers may continue to invest in projects which yield only a fraction of the nonguaranteed investments. Thus, the federal government is actively subsidizing inefficient investments which reduces the productivity of the nation's capital stock and consequently lowers the rate of economic growth. The slower rate of economic growth is, of course, accompanied by higher inflation and higher unemployment.

As an example of how private sector investments are crowded out in favor of governmentally sponsored investments consider the following: In 1980 when a 20 percent prime rate and 16 percent consumer loan rate contributed to the bankruptcy of thousands of small businesses such as auto dealerships and grocery stores, the Rural Electrification Administration began a new program to provide 35-year loans at five percent interest to finance rural cable television systems; rural home mortgages were available at 3.3 percent; and insured student loans went for seven percent, to name just a few. Also during that year, while many private utilities were paying 16 percent on their long-term bonds, the TVA was borrowing at a rate several percentage points lower. As a result of this and other subsidies, the cost of electricity supplied by the TVA is lower than in many areas served by less favored private companies. In 1979, for example, TVA rates were about 50 percent lower than in such Frostbelt states as New York and Massachusetts and about 38 percent below the national average.[9]

It is very difficult, if not impossible, to gauge the extent of crowding out caused by federal loan guarantees, but some preliminary estimates have been made. Economist Herbert M. Kaufman of the University of Arizona conducted an empirical study of federal loan guarantees in which he estimated that for every $1 billion in loan guarantees, between

[9]As cited in R. Utt, "Federal Lending Programs," testimony before the Senate Committee on Banking, Housing, and Urban Affairs, October 7, 1981.

$736 million and $1.32 billion in private investment is crowded out.[10] These are rough estimates, but they nevertheless indicate that loan guarantees which are being extended at a rate of over $100 billion per year are sure to have a profound negative impact on economic growth, employment, and inflation. The effect on inflation is not likely to be very significant, however, since changes in aggregate output occur relatively slowly as a result of reductions in private investment spending. However, the potential exists that the upward pressure on interest rates caused by federal intrusion into the credit markets via loan guarantees may bring pressure to bear on the Federal Reserve to "accommodate" the Treasury by expanding the money supply, thereby reinflating the economy.

A somewhat more subtle way in which federal loan guarantees are used to exert government control over the allocation of resources without explicit budgetary entries is the exercise of various forms of influence over the recipients of the subsidies. For example, the Federal Housing Administration, which administers the largest loan guarantee program, attempts to implement various social policies by vetoing a loan application if a builder does not comply with FHA's regulations on marketing to minority groups, environmental impact statements, architectural review, underwriting minimum wages, and so on. Because of the division of responsibility for all these objectives, considerable confusion and delay arises, which increases the cost of housing construction. Further, once a firm or an industry is dependent upon financial assistance from the government, this is often used as a lever to impose additional regulatory controls which may be totally unrelated to the government's contingent liability. Current efforts by some members of the executive and legislative branches of the federal government to deregulate the private sector in order to foster more rapid economic growth are sure to be confounded somewhat by the regulatory requirements that accompany the rapidly growing volume of loan guarantees.

A closer look at the pervasive influence of the federal government through its loan guarantee programs is provided by the data in Table 29. Housing and agriculture, two of the strongest political constituencies in the nation, dominate the field, accounting for over 80 percent of all loan guarantees. In 1980 the use of guaranteed loans for housing was nine times greater than the use of direct loans, with 43 separate

[10]Herbert M. Kaufman, "Loan Guarantees and Crowding Out," in Congressional Budget Office, *Economics of Federal Credit Activity* (Washington, D.C.: CBO, April 1980), pp. 35–39.

Table 29

GUARANTEED LOAN TRANSACTIONS OF THE FEDERAL
GOVERNMENT, 1981
(millions of dollars)

Agency or Program	Guaranteed Loans
PRESIDENTIAL APPROPRIATIONS	
International security assistance	2,505
International development assistance	105
AGRICULTURE	
Farmers Home Administration	15,329
Commodity Credit Corporation export credit	1,516
Rural Electrification Administration	4,793
COMMERCE	
Economic development assistance	178
National Oceanic and Atmospheric Administration	31
Energy research and technology	1,278
DEFENSE: military	1
HEALTH AND HUMAN SERVICES	
Health programs	69
HOUSING AND URBAN DEVELOPMENT	
Subsidized low-rent public housing	16,968
Federal Housing Administration	17,742
Community development	45
GNMA: mortgage-backed securities	16,853
INTERIOR: Indian programs	1
TRANSPORTATION	
Rail programs	104
Washington M.T.A. bonds	—
Federal ship financing fund	928
Aircraft loans	429
TREASURY	
Guarantees of New York City notes	300
Chrysler Corporation loan guarantee program	400
Biomass energy development	—
NASA: Long-term satellite leases	111
VETERANS ADMINISTRATION: housing	10,354

Table 29 cont.

Agency or Program	Guaranteed Loans
EXPORT-IMPORT BANK	4,899
FOUNDATION FOR EDUCATION ASSISTANCE	
Guarantees of SLMA debt issues	1,955
Student loan insurance form	7,762
Government Services Administration	14
NATIONAL CREDIT UNION ADMINISTRATION	85
SMALL BUSINESS ADMINISTRATION	
Business loan guarantees	2,986
Disaster loan fund	1
Pollution control bond guarantees	100
Tennessee Valley Authority	3,624
OTHER AGENCIES & PROGRAMS	14

SOURCE: *Budget of the United States Government, Special Analyses,* "Federal Credit Programs," Appendix F, 1982.

programs. The Export-Import Bank (which subsidizes selected American exporters), student loan programs, and the Small Business Administration also administer a large volume of guaranteed lending, which amounted to approximately $16 billion in 1980.

Equity Aspects of Federal Loan Guarantees

In addition to fostering a less efficient allocation of resources and hindering economic growth, many of the loan guarantee programs listed in Table 29 would be considered by many to be inequitable. An extreme case in point is the student loan program which, with few eligibility requirements, creates generous subsidies for higher-income households. With such loans available to students and their parents at seven percent interest regardless of financial need, the high market interest rates of the late 1970s and early 1980s have provided many lucrative investment opportunities for wealthy families. As the spread between interest rates on student loans and market rates widened, new student loans rose from $2.7 billion in 1979 to $7.2 billion in 1981, reflecting a widespread recognition of the opportunities to borrow thousands of dollars at seven percent and invest the proceeds in long-term bonds or money market funds paying 14–16 percent.[11] Furthermore, hundreds of millions of dollars in student loans are now in default, rendering these loans outright gifts to the students and their parents.

The vast majority of federal loan guarantee programs provide subsidies to individuals who are not generally considered to be financially disadvantaged, regardless of the rhetoric associated with such programs. There is a very strong incentive for the administrators of loan guarantee programs to subsidize politically powerful groups, regardless of income, who will, in return, provide support for the agency at appropriations time. Consider the fact that even though HUD's chief goals are supposedly "the elimination of substandard and inadequate housing through the clearance of slums and blighted areas" it has established hundreds of programs which have nothing to do with slum clearance. For example, HUD's housing rehabilitation loan program has extended three percent guaranteed loans to individuals earning over $50,000 per year to finance skylights and greenhouses.[12]

In sum, if there is a pattern of behavior guiding the granting of loan guarantees by the federal government, it is based upon the ability of the subsidized group to provide political support for the agency and certainly not efficiency or equity considerations.[13] Eliminating many, if not all, loan guarantees would inflict short-term losses on specially privileged groups, but would increase the productivity of the nation's capital stock and limit the negative-sum transfers of wealth to higher-income groups, which all come at the expense of the general public.

Debt Collection, Default, and Debudgeting the Budget

The huge indirect costs of federal loan guarantees and off-budget lending are accompanied by billions of dollars of direct costs in the form of loan defaults. When a borrower defaults, the loan or loan guarantee then becomes a gift to the borrower and, simultaneously, a

[11]*Budget of the U.S. Government, Special Analyses,* various years.

[12]As reported in D. Lambro, *Fat City: How Washington Wastes Your Taxes* (South Bend, Ind: Regnery Co. 1980), p. 128.

[13]When both inefficiency and inequity are widely acknowledged, loan guarantees are often justified on national security grounds. In hearings before the Senate Banking Committee on October 7, 1981, on the subject of loan guarantees to Exxon and Tasco corporations for a shale oil project, a Department of Defense official testified that shale oil development and, consequently, the loan guarantee for Exxon and Tasco, was urgently needed to enhance the strategic oil reserve. Senator Harrison Schmidt of New Mexico discredited that viewpoint, however, by mentioning that shale oil was far more expensive than conventional oil, and was therefore a bad deal from a national defense standpoint.

way in which the federal largesse can be distributed without undergoing the scrutiny of the appropriations process. History shows that many federal credit programs appear to be designed to do exactly that.

It is very difficult, if not impossible, to obtain an accurate account of the volume of loan defaults, for federal agencies are reluctant to make such data available. In 1979, the General Accounting Office (GAO) conducted a limited survey of debts owed the federal government and found that by the end of 1978 over $140 billion in overdue loans was outstanding, a $22 billion increase over the previous year.[14] One GAO auditor stated, "I'd say we're losing about a half billion dollars a year in bad debts that go uncollected."

GAO surveyed 12 federal agencies and found that most do not even attempt to collect many of their debts: Nine major agencies simply wrote off $428 million in uncollected debts in 1978, and many agencies don't even report their "uncollectibles" at all. When federal agencies do attempt to collect their debts, they are notoriously inefficient and slow in doing so. For example, GAO found that one federal agency which kept data on debt collection costs spent $8.72 per account in 1976 compared to a large commercial agency in the United States which averaged $3.50 per account for the same function. Private firms surveyed by GAO stated that it is profitable to attempt to collect debts as small as $25 to the point in the collection process where a decision is made on whether to seek a court judgment. By contrast, in 1977 most federal agencies simply wrote off debts up to $600. In one instance, an individual could afford a $170,000 mortgage, but the Veterans Administration wrote off his $638 debt as "uncollectible." Whenever the federal government does follow through with seeking a court judgment, it takes a minimum of one year to reach the court stage, compared to about five months for private firms surveyed by GAO. Among the agencies failing to collect debts are the Small Business Administration, the Veterans Administration, and the Farmers Home Administration, which wrote off $274 million in bad debts in 1978, a 66 percent increase from 1976 figures.

[14]U.S. General Accounting Office, *The Government Can Be More Productive in Collecting its Debts by Following Commercial Practices* (Washington, D.C.: U.S. Government Printing Office, February 23, 1979). GAO recently reported that the number of foreign governments in default for loan guarantees to purchase military supplies increased from two in 1978 to 13 as of February 1982. This type of guarantee permits Congress to extend military aid to selected countries without going through the appropriations process and being subjected to wide publicity. See Dan Morgan, "13 Arms Buyers in Default on Interest to U.S.," *Washington Post*, July 17, 1982, p. 1.

149

The SBA has a particularly high default rate, and for good reason—a loan applicant must prove that he is *not* credit-worthy in order to qualify! A borrower is eligible for a direct SBA loan only if he can prove he was turned down by at least two banks *and* that his loan is too risky for even SBA's loan guarantee program. The SBA direct loan program wrote off $166 million in loans in 1980, which was topped by the SBA's $368 million in guaranteed loan defaults during that year.[15]

The Office of Education (now the Department of Education) was another agency surveyed by GAO which had severe debt collection problems. Defaulted guaranteed student loans soared from $52 million in 1974 to $1.7 billion in 1982, a 3,300 percent increase in just eight years. The Department also had a collection problem with direct loans. As of July 1982, an estimated 1.2 million students had defaulted on direct loans amounting to about $600 million. The federal government has actively encouraged students to believe in the student loan Santa Claus by recently passing legislation making it illegal for personal credit checks to make any mention of student loan defaults. Surely if the Congress had any intention of collecting these debts, it would not have passed this law and would not permit the SBA to virtually guarantee itself a high default rate.

In sum, billions of dollars of loans and loan guarantees which distribute indirect off-budget subsidies are being turned into direct gifts by simply not enforcing the terms of the loan. Furthermore, it is difficult to believe that members of Congress did not intend for the system to work that way, for it is in their self-interest that it do so.

Federally Sponsored Off-Budget Enterprises

A third category of federal off-budget operations consists of "government-sponsored enterprises," of which there are many. The major types of federally sponsored OBEs are those which engage in credit activity. Included among them are the Federal National Mortgage Association (FNMA), the Farm Credit Administration (FCA), the Federal Home Loan Bank (FHLB), the Federal Home Loan Mortgage Corporation (FHLMC), and the Student Loan Marketing Association (SLMA). These agencies were at one time on-budget, but their large and rapidly expanding borrowings became an embarrassment to some members of Congress and were omitted from the budget in 1968.[16] Although now

---

[15]Hardin and Denzau, *The Unrestrained Growth of Federal Credit Programs,* p. 25.

[16]*Budget of the U.S. Government, Special Analyses,* Appendix E, "Borrowing and Debt," 1982.

privately owned, they are subject to government supervision and by law must consult with the Treasury Department in planning the marketing of their debt. In addition, many of their board members are presidential appointees, and various decisions must be cleared by other government agencies as well as the Treasury. For example, many of the FNMA's decisions must be approved by the Secretary of HUD. These agencies are also granted special preferences and certain tax exemptions. Such attributes permit federally sponsored OBEs to borrow funds for governmentally authorized purposes at rates only slightly above the Treasury's own rates and lend the money to certain specified groups. Thus, federally sponsored enterprises are private in name only, and are yet another way in which the federal government directs the allocation of billions of dollars of credit without being subject to the federal budget review process. The special assistance granted federally sponsored enterprises also hinders the development of private firms which would compete in performing these same tasks more efficiently. A case in point is the FNMA, which in 1980 owned $56 billion in mortgages with an average life of over 14 years and an average yield of about 9.5 percent.[17] While betting on long-term rates to drop, "Fannie Mae" relied heavily on short-term financing, accumulating $17 billion in short-term debt that must be rolled over within a year. About half of that $17 billion was costing Fannie Mae 17 percent, with the rest at around 9.7 percent, but that would have to be refinanced at about 17 percent. Consequently, Fannie Mae lost $146 million in the first half of 1981. Despite these huge losses, it has had no trouble in rolling over its debt which has been trading at less than a percentage point above short-term Treasury bills. The reason for this, of course, is the implicit (and explicit) guarantee of the federal government. Fannie Mae has the right, by law, to ask the Treasury to purchase $2.5 billion of its debt to provide liquidity! Unlike a private firm, which bears the brunt of hundreds of millions of dollars in losses, Fannie Mae and the other federally sponsored OBEs are protected from such losses and therefore have weak incentives to do anything about them.

The total estimated volume of borrowing by federally sponsored enterprises during 1980–1983 is shown in Table 30. Estimated borrowing is expected to nearly double by 1983, to a total of over $52 billion, with $315 billion in debt outstanding at that time. This would continue the recent trend of a very rapid expansion in borrowing by federally sponsored enterprises which, up until 1974, had never borrowed more

[17]A. Sloan, "Saving Fannie," *Forbes*, October 26, 1981, pp. 54–55.

151

Table 30

BORROWING BY FEDERALLY SPONSORED ENTERPRISES
(millions of dollars)

Description	Borrowing or Repayment (−)				Debt Outstanding at End of 1983 (est.)
	1980	1981	1982 (est.)	1983 (est.)	
Housing and Urban Development:					
Federal National Mortgage Association	6,347	4,342	11,646	11,657	79,991
Farm Credit Administration:*					
Banks for Cooperatives	1,542	737	1,093	1,126	11,351
Federal Intermediate Credit Banks	3,536	1,921	2,882	3,502	27,666
Federal Land Banks	7,076	6,819	6,842	7,494	55,411
Federal Home Loan Bank Board:					
Federal Home Loan Banks	6,454	21,029	3,662	4,075	65,365
Federal Home Loan Mortgage Corporation	3,141	1,847	20,948	23,460	67,752
Foundation for Education Assistance:					
Student Loan Marketing Association	1,070	2,223	1,603	1,543	7,713
Total	29,165	38,917	48,676	52,867	315,249
Less increase in holdings of debt issued by government-sponsored enterprises	1,691	230	− 882	− 500	3,170
Total borrowing by government-sponsored enterprises	27,473	38,687	49,558	53,367	312,079

*The debt represented by consolidated bonds is attributed to the respective Farm Credit Banks.
SOURCE: *Budget of the U.S. Government, Special Analyses,* Appendix E, "Borrowing and Debt," 1982.

than $14.9 billion annually. This amount increased sharply to $24.1 billion by 1978 and exceeded $38 billion in 1981. Thus, during periods of high and rising interest rates which crowded out many private-sector borrowers, federally sponsored and controlled borrowing expanded at a rapid pace. Nearly three-fourths of all federally sponsored borrowing during the 1981–83 period will be used to support the mortgage market. As one senator has said, it seems as though the federal government is trying to make everyone a "preferred borrower" of some sort these days.

There are numerous other federally sponsored enterprises throughout the country which provide various services to federally specified constituent groups but bypass the federal appropriations process. Two of the best known examples are the TVA and the Bonneville Power Administration, both federally chartered OBEs, which obtain most of their funds by issuing revenue bonds but are also the recipients of federal grants and some appropriations.

Fiscal Discipline and Government Regulation

Off-budget activities are by no means the only way in which balanced budget or tax/expenditure limitation requirements have been evaded by federal politicians. Politicians can subsidize a particular group without resorting to the appropriations process by enacting various forms of "sweetheart legislation." For example, import quotas on automobiles (or any other product) would restrict the supply of automobiles, increasing the prices paid by consumers and the profits of the owners of the auto industry. The effect is the same as a tax-financed subsidy— a special interest benefits at the expense of the general public. Government regulation provides myriad ways to conduct business-as-usual regardless of budgetary restrictions.

A second type of regulation that is used to achieve the ends of politicians and entails significant non-budgeted costs is the direct regulation of industry by various agencies such as the Interstate Commerce Commission (ICC), the Federal Trade Commission (FTC), and the Federal Communications Commission (FCC). Politically influential groups such as the trucking industry, the airline industry, and labor unions have used these agencies to restrict competition and increase profits and wages. For example, with the sanction of the ICC, trucking firms have been able to act as a cartel in setting their rates. Representatives of the regulated firms meet periodically to set freight rates. These "rate bureaus" have been specifically exempted from the antitrust laws pertaining to price-fixing. The Teamsters Union has also benefited from the ICC's policies of entry restriction, because such restrictions prevent non-union firms from entering the industry and competing for traffic carried by unionized firms. Consequently, the Teamsters have been able to raise the wages of their drivers to a level about 50 percent higher than those in the unregulated sector.[18] This type of regulation, which is quite pervasive, imposes great burdens on taxpayers and consumers even though there are no budgetary entries to reflect such costs. Also, special interest groups spend millions of dollars each year lobbying for preferential treatment; such expenses are an added cost to society since the resources could have been used to produce additional goods and services, rather than merely redistribute income.[19]

A third way in which government conducts its business without explicitly taxing or spending is by regulating the day-to-day activities of businesses with regard to working conditions, finances, consumer safety, the environment, hiring practices, and so on. Although these regulatory activities may or may not result in diminished competition in various industries, they surely impose enormous costs on taxpayers in return for sometimes questionable benefits. Economist Murray Weidenbaum conservatively estimated that the direct, measurable cost of federal regulation of business was $102.7 billion in 1979, of which only $4.8 billion, or approximately five percent, was budgeted as administrative costs; the remaining $97.9 billion was the cost of compliance, which was largely paid by consumers.[20]

Regulation and Labor

Government regulation has major allocative and distributive effects not only on product markets, but also on labor markets.[21] Occupational licensing requirements, for example, are a means of subsidizing special interest groups without resorting to explicit taxation. One well-known example of the effects of licensing is the regulation of the taxicab business. In New York City a license costing $65,000 must be purchased to own and operate a cab. Consequently, the supply of taxi services is

[18]Rayburn M. Williams, *Inflation: Money, Jobs, and Politicians* (Arlington Heights, Ill.: AHM Publishers, 1980), p. 105.

[19]These lobbying activities have been termed "rent seeking" and are discussed in detail in James Buchanan, Robert Tollison, and Gordon Tullock, eds., *Toward a Theory of the Rent-Seeking Society* (College Station: Texas A&M Press, 1980).

[20]Murray Weidenbaum, *The Future of Business Regulation* (New York: American Management Association, 1979).

[21]For a discussion of labor market regulation see James T. Bennett, Dan C. Heldman, and Manuel H. Johnson, *Deregulating Labor Relations* (Dallas: The Fisher Institute, 1981).

severely restricted, increasing cab fares to the benefit of existing drivers at the expense of potential drivers and customers. The effects are similar in other industries as a result of more than 3,000 statutory provisions requiring licenses for such diverse occupations as fortune-telling, funeral directing, and the practice of medicine.[22]

A second way in which government regulation of labor markets redistributes wealth is through enforcement of the minimum wage law. It is a well-established empirical fact that, regardless of good intentions, the effect of the minimum wage law is to hurt precisely the group that the law is supposed to help—those with the least skills, seniority, and income.[23] If an unskilled worker, for example, can contribute $2.50 per hour to a firm's profits, and the law mandates a $3.50-per-hour minimum wage, it will be more profitable for the firm not to hire the unskilled worker. Thus, increases in the minimum wage are accompanied by increased unemployment of unskilled workers, predominantly teenagers. The major beneficiaries of the minimum wage law are politicians who can convince people they are doing something positive about unemployment and poverty, relatively skilled workers who retain their jobs at the higher (minimum) wage, and members of labor unions who, being relatively skilled, compete with unskilled, non-union labor. It is difficult to believe that labor unions in California, for example, advocate the enforcement of minimum wage laws to non-union migrant workers because of altruism rather than a desire to price migrant workers out of the market.

"Equal employment opportunity" regulation also can affect the allocation of labor resources. One example is the equal-pay-for-equal-work rule, which most likely *increases* employment discrimination. If an employer discriminates by paying male workers $10 an hour and equally qualified female workers $5 an hour, in a competitive labor market the firm's female workers will be bid away at wages greater than $5 an hour. Eventually, all of the firm's female labor will be bid away, leaving the firm at a competitive disadvantage and reducing its profits. Thus, in an unregulated labor market, discrimination is costly to employers. Equal-pay-for-equal-work rules lower the costs of discrimination in employment since an employer's profits are no longer affected by passing over equally qualified women to hire men. Therefore, enforcement of such laws will more likely lead to more, not less discrimination.

[22]Walter E. Williams, "Government Sanctioned Restraints That Reduce Economic Opportunities for Minorities," *Policy Review*, Fall 1977, pp. 1–29.

[23]Bennett, et al., *Deregulating Labor Relations*, pp. 86–98.

American labor unions comprised mostly of white males are among the most vocal advocates of equal-pay-for-equal-work laws, and it is hard to believe that this concern is based on altruism. Labor unions in South Africa have similarly lobbied intensely for such laws, and openly admitted that the reason for doing so is because government programs "no longer protected the white worker."[24]

Finally, government also influences labor market outcomes by enhancing the market power of labor unions through the National Labor Relations Board (NLRB). A recent study has shown that the NLRB's regulation of collective bargaining has greatly enhanced the power of labor unions at the expense of those who are barred from employment by unions as well as consumers who pay the price of reduced economic efficiency and higher inflation.[25] The social cost of NLRB regulation was estimated to be at least $22 billion in 1979. Overall, the total social cost of labor market regulation was estimated to have been $170.3 billion in 1979.

In addition to off-budget activities, their existing regulatory mechanisms permit politicians to affect the allocation of hundreds of billions of dollars of resources without taxing or spending. The predominant activity of government, the redistribution of wealth from the general public to special interest groups, is conducted through extensive regulation of product and labor markets, which requires administrative expenses that are trivial when compared to the social cost of regulation, and is carried on at all levels of government.

Some Concluding Observations

Following the precedents established at the state and local levels of government, the federal government has evaded constraints on its spending and taxing activities largely through credit market activity conducted via off-budget agencies such as the Federal Financing Bank, the issuance of hundreds of billions of dollars in loan guarantees, and the activities of privately owned, but governmentally controlled, enterprises such as Fannie Mae. The advent of the Budget Reform Act of 1974 and the taxpayer revolt of the 1970s has led to a tremendous expansion in the off-budget activities of the federal government so that of total federal credit outlays of $155.8 billion in 1982, fully 82 percent ($127.7 billion) was in the form of either off-budget loans or guaranteed loans, neither of which are fully reflected in the budget document or

[24]Williams, p. 11.
[25]Bennett, et al., pp. 112–19.

156

undergo budgetary review by the Congress. In addition, borrowing by government-sponsored enterprises is estimated to approach $50 billion in 1982 so that the federal government will be responsible for over 40 percent of all credit advanced in U.S. credit markets in that year, compared to an 11-percent participation rate in 1969.[26] Even though many have treated off-budget federal credit activity as though it constituted the proverbial free lunch, the crowding out of the private sector and the subsidization of economically inefficient, but politically popular, investment projects will surely lead to slower economic growth, higher unemployment, and, possibly, higher inflation.

In addition to off-budget credit activities, government regulation is another way of accomplishing the ends of politicians without explicitly appropriating funds. In principle, anything that can be accomplished through the taxing and spending aspects of the budget can be accomplished instead through regulation.

As pressures for a balanced budget and restrictions on federal spending mount, one may expect an accelerated use of the federal government's off-budget mechanisms. The proposed balanced budget amendment to the U.S. Constitution (S.J.Res. 58) does take into consideration the activities of the FFB and proposes to include them within the budget. The proposed amendment does not, however, address the larger problems created by loan guarantees, federally sponsored enterprises, and regulation and should therefore be seen as only a first step in the direction of fiscal responsibility, but not necessarily a major one. Attempts to reduce the extent of off-budget credit activity have had little success. In the 1981 credit budget, President Reagan proposed that direct loans increase by only 1.7 percent and loan guarantees by 8.3 percent. By the time the President's 1982 budget was published, however, it showed that loans had increased by 21 percent, while loan guarantees rose by an estimated 31 percent. Formally including *all* federal credit activities in the congressional budget process is likely to improve our ability to put a cap on seemingly runaway federal spending and borrowing, although even more imaginative financing schemes would surely follow. Even when federal loan guarantees are effectively curtailed, there is the possibility that the cost of these programs will merely be shifted to lower levels of government, rather than reduced. Recently, the Reagan administration has attempted to cut the federal government's $6 billion student aid program by limiting loan guaran-

[26]*Budget of the U.S. Government, Special Analyses*, Appendix F, "Federal Credit Programs," 1982, p. 6.

tees to lower- and middle-income families earning less than $30,000 per year. In response to these proposals, Dartmouth College, Harvard, Northwestern University, and over 100 other universities either created off-budget "educational finance authorities" or made use of existing OBEs, which have issued revenue bonds to finance student loans.[27] At present, at least five states—New Hampshire, Massachusetts, Maine, Illinois, and Iowa—have established newly created OBEs, and four other states—New York, Maryland, Pennsylvania, and Florida—have legislation pending that would establish more of such authorities. Tactics such as this are sure to confound attempts to constrain government credit activity and should be considered by citizens and policymakers seeking to do so.

[27]R. Bucklin, "Colleges Aid Students With Bonds," *Washington Post*, July 2, 1982, p. C-9.

158

VIII. OBEs Overseas

In the context of political decision-making and, in fact, in all decision-making, the forces of rational self-interest are timeless and know no boundaries. The politician's penchant for excessive spending has been well known for thousands of years and has long been recognized as a serious problem threatening the freedom of democratic countries worldwide. Not surprisingly, attempts at constraining government taxing and spending powers have spawned the development of underground governments in numerous other countries. The off-budget "margins of the state" are quite active in countries such as Great Britain, Japan, and Israel, to name a few, and have greatly expanded the scope of governmental control of the economies of those countries.

OBEs in the United Kingdom

To shield government activities from the British taxpayer's scrutiny, over 3,000 "quasi-autonomous non-governmental organizations" (quangos) perform various tasks ranging from the activities of the Working Group on Rickets to those of the Commission for Racial Equality and the Port of London Authority. Broadly defined, a quango is a government-sponsored entity created by parliamentary ministers and given special powers. There are more than 30,000 bureaucrats, or "quangurus," who are appointed by parliamentary ministers to administer these agencies who were paid £3,320,000 plus expenses in 1979.[1] Although they receive government appropriations, quangos are rarely subjected to any parliamentary overview and are accountable only to the minister who hires, fires, and pays the managerial appointees. Of the more than 3,000 quangos only about 70 are required to have their accounts audited by the Comptroller or Auditor General, which renders the large majority of them financially unaccountable to Parliament.

There are several methods for creating quangos. First, and most common, is primary legislation, wherein an act of Parliament establishes a quango, sets out its functions, and prescribes how and by

---

[1]Phillip Holland, *The Governance of Quangos* (London: Adam Smith Institute, 1981).

whom its board of directors is to be appointed. Second, there are Royal Charters and Royal Warrants, which have created such bodies as the Research Councils and the Sports Council. A third method is through secondary legislation, which authorizes a minister to establish a quango by regulation.

Quangos enable British politicians to greatly expand their patronage opportunities and to exert more influence over public policy than they would by following parliamentary procedures. For example, after the first five years of the Labour Party's government in the 1970s, nearly all the important quango appointments were held by supporters of the Labour Party. Prominent union leaders held as many as eight or 10 appointments each. Thus, even when a political party is ousted at the polls in Britain, it can still exert considerable control, as is starkly evidenced by the activities of one prominent quango, the National Enterprise Board (NEB). The Board was established in 1975 with the authorization "to assist or maintain or reorganize any industrial under-taking and extend public ownership into profitable areas of manufac-turing industry; to promote industrial democracy in undertakings which it controls and to hold and manage such public property as may be vested in it."[2] The implications of this for British citizens, plagued for decades with the burden of subsidizing dozens of lethargic nationalized industries, are ominous. The National Enterprise Board, through its extensive borrowing powers, can steadily pursue the socialists' goal of government control of the means of production without any recourse to the Parliament. From 1975 to 1979 the Board took over numerous private firms. The newly elected Conservative Party government forced it to halt its acquisition activities, but the NEB remains intact and therefore remains a threat to free enterprise in Great Britain.

Among the most influential quangos are the scores of supervisory or regulatory bodies which issue directives that "must be obeyed" but are nevertheless not accountable to Parliament. The exact details of how these agencies operate are not of particular importance here, but their general effect has been succinctly stated by one parliamentary minister:

> The nation has in recent years become increasingly subject to com-mands, instructions, and 'advice that must be obeyed' . . . covering every aspect of life, work and leisure. Thus, teachers receive instruc-tions on how to do their work from the Equal Opportunities Com-mission. The Football Association is given advice on running its leisure centers by the Commission for Racial Equality. There are advisory committees to tell us which wrecks are historical, to devise bigger and

[2]Ibid., p. 28.

more demanding statistical forms, to advise us where and when to spend our holidays, to protect us from our own fecklessness and carelessness, to tell us if we may pull down our houses, to instruct us on how we must train workers and how we must behave when at work. . . . Many of the bodies were created without prior approval or even knowledge of Parliament. However, Parliament itself was to blame for the establishment by statute of the biggest and most powerful independent government agencies.[3]

Quasi-Judicial Quangos

Another category of quango is comprised of those which serve a quasi-judicial function, thereby usurping some of the functions of the independent judiciary in Britain. As one example, the Advisory Conciliation and Arbitration Service (ACAS) was established in 1975 and charged in general with "promoting the improvement of industrial relations," and, in particular, with "encouraging the extension of collective bargaining." The ACAS was made up entirely of people with trade union backgrounds and was responsible for adjudicating all disputes regarding trade union issues. With the aid of another quango, the Central Arbitration Committee, ACAS could also enforce its decisions. Needless to say, the purpose and effect of the ACAS is to bypass both the Parliament and the independent judiciary, and to grant labor unionists the legal power to enforce collective bargaining decisions themselves. This would be analogous to giving Lane Kirkland, president of the AFL-CIO, the legal right to decide all collective bargaining disputes in whatever way he saw fit.

Other quasi-judicial quangos abound in Britain, and serve similar purposes. Among the most active and most publicized is the Commission for Racial Equality (CRE), which in 1975 was created by combining the Race Relations Board, a political pressure group for ethnic minorities, with the Community Relations Commission, which has enforcement powers. Thus, the CRE gives a small political pressure group the legal right to make binding decisions on whether certain practices are "discriminatory"—hardly the type of impartiality one expects from the courts. In sum, quasi-judicial quangos are a mechanism through which individual parliamentary ministers can distribute government-sanctioned empowerments to special interest groups to enable them to transfer wealth to themselves legally, and without recourse to either the Parliament or the independent judiciary.

[3]Ibid., p. 21.

"Taxation Without Representation" Returns to Great Britain

Although no attempts have been made to measure the regulatory costs of "government by quangocracy" in Britain, they are sure to be large, and to stifle the vitality of the British economy. Furthermore, the activities of quangos crowd out many private enterprises, forcing British citizens to pay for higher-priced goods and services produced by inherently less efficient "public" enterprises. None of these costs or activities are subjected to parliamentary or judicial scrutiny, and they are imposed on British citizens despite, rather than as a result of, representative democracy in Great Britain.

Government by quango blatantly ignores the old axiom that there should be no taxation without representation. Many quangos, such as the water authorities, are granted taxing powers by statute. The water authorities levy charges based on the value of property they serve rather than the cost of service. Similarly, Industrial Training Boards levy taxes on those private companies which must comply with their edicts.

It is clear that the underground government in Great Britain is very large, indicating that Britain has travelled even further down the "road to serfdom" than most would realize. Quangos have been used to avoid constraints on government powers imposed by the normal workings of parliamentary democracy in Britain. The growth of the underground government in Britain has been rapid, especially in the past 15 years, and has been nonpartisan. In the first two years after the Conservative Party's victory in 1979, at least 55 new quangos were established by Conservative ministers.[4]

The British experience provides a valuable lesson to those citizens who would like to constrain the size and growth of the governmental leviathan. Many of the off-budget enterprises at the state and local levels of government in the United States were patterned after one of the oldest British OBEs, the Port of London Authority. It would be most unfortunate if government by quango were also added to the list of British imports to the U.S.

Japanese OBEs

In every post office in Japan hangs a poster reading, "The funds you deposit in the postal savings system are invested in public corporations and banks, starting with your own town or village, and they serve to

---

[4]Oliver Pritchett, "How to Survive the 'Quango' Hunting Season," London *Sunday Telegraph*, May 24, 1981.

make your town or village a better place to live."[5] The Japanese Ministry of Finance has developed a scheme whereby savings accounts established at post offices and other trust funds deposited with the government are placed into a so-called "second budget," known as the Fiscal Investment and Loan Plan (FILP). It is called a plan because it involves a large measure of central government direction of the economy through various "public corporations," and the word "plan" disguises its status as a budget. There is also a third budget, known as the "special accounts," which is oriented toward special projects which Japanese politicians would like to detach from the appropriations process for the main, general account budget.

The creation of these two additional budgets was the result of the principle of maintaining balanced or even surplus budgets, which became firmly established in Japanese political culture during the post-war years, until it eventually eroded during the late 1960s. The creation of these devices enabled Japanese politicians to claim fiscal responsibility while taking greater control over society's resources through these alternative budgets, which are more isolated from taxpayer scrutiny than the general account budget. The FILP was created in 1953 when it constituted 33.4 percent of the general account budget and 4.5 percent of GNP. By 1973 it had grown to about 50 percent of the general account and 6.3 percent of GNP. The FILP budget is used to finance Japan's "public corporations," of which there are hundreds, and is administered by the bureaucrats in the Financial Bureau of the Ministry of Finance. The reasons for establishing these public corporations were succinctly stated in a recent book-length treatment of their activities:

> A government . . . may set up a public corporation to insulate an activity from parliamentary or bureaucratic politics, or to draw capital and technology into an area that is too risky or unprofitable to attract private enterprise. On the other hand, public corporations also have been known to serve as post-retirement havens for bureaucrats, as dummies to camouflage government activities in sensitive areas, as ways for special interests to gain indirect access to the public treasury, and as political compromises when the interests of government and private capital clash.[6]

Thus, it appears that the much-heralded Japan, Inc. is deeply involved in political patronage, the subsidization of inefficient or failing indus-

---

[5]As cited in Chalmers Johnson, *Japan's Public Policy Companies* (Washington, D.C.: American Enterprise Institute, 1978).

[6]Ibid., p. 25.

tries, and evasion of the budgetary process—a surefire prescription for eventual economic stagnation.

Japanese OBEs vary widely in their activities and perform many functions, including the provision of many goods and services that would otherwise have been provided by regular government departments or by more efficient private firms. There are five "direct government enterprises" as such: the postal service, the forestry service, the government printer (including currency and stamps), the mint, and a government monopoly of the manufacture of industrial alcohol. The predominant type of Japanese OBE, however, is the Special Legal Entity (SLE), of which there are over 3,000, which expend over 80 percent of the FILP budget. SLEs perform myriad functions which affect every aspect of Japanese life, from the construction of housing, roads, airports, and ships to banking, education, and even the distribution of groceries. Among the most publicized SLEs is the Japanese National Railways Corporation (JNRC), which is currently running a deficit equivalent to 18 percent of the general account budget.[7] Some SLEs must subject their budgets to review by some members of the legislature, but others, such as those in the category called the Kodan, are subject only to the approval of their supervising ministers. Consequently, the Kodan, which invest huge sums in public works and construction projects, are the most active of all SLEs. The Kodan produce such items as apartment houses (by the Japan Housing Corporation), ships, seaports, and water projects and issue revenue bonds to partially finance many of these projects.

An example of the type of SLE that serves to subsidize failing or inefficient businesses is the Koko, which claims to "guide the economy by making indicative loans." The Koko make loans on the basis of so-called policy interest rates—intended for clients proposing projects which are unprofitable or too risky to have access to other sources of capital. Thus, the Koko provide Japanese politicians with a means of bypassing the normal legislative process so that more investments are made by political rather than economic criteria, which will ultimately stunt Japanese economic growth.

Another major category of SLE which imposes an indirect, but major, cost on Japanese citizens is the Tokashu Karsha, which controls prices in various industries. For example, when customers of the chemical fertilizer industry complained that the industry, in trying to be com-

[7]Peter F. Drucker, "Clouds Forming Across the Japanese Sun," *Wall Street Journal*, July 13, 1982, p. 28.

164

petitive in world markets, was exporting ammonium sulfate at prices lower than what was charged to domestic farmers, the Ministry of International Trade and Industry (MITI) established the Japan Ammonium Sulfate Export Company. The company buys all the ammonium sulfate produced in the country, sells what is demanded at fixed domestic prices, and exports the rest. MITI's stated purpose in setting up the company was "to force rationalization on the industry and end cutthroat competition."[8] The words "irrational" and "cutthroat" are often used to describe free-market competition by those political agents who benefit personally by setting prices in a way that benefits various special interests at the expense of the general public. Thus, in some ways the regulatory situation in Japan is little different from that in the U.S.

Political Patronage and the Japanese Bureaucracy

The growth of government bureaucracies is a hallmark of all democratic countries in the past century, and Japan is no exception. One reason for the growth of bureaucracy is that such growth tends to be self-generating.[9] An increase in the number of bureaucrats strengthens the political power of bureaucrats to lobby for higher wages and benefits, which pulls even more people into the public sector, who combine with the original participants to lobby for even further wage increases. But there is a problem with this process from the perspective of the government bureaucrat. Beyond some point, a larger bureaucracy may mean smaller benefits to existing bureaucrats who would prefer not to share the "wage pie" with any more workers who may, at some point, provide only very marginal political support for a larger pie.[10] The Japanese bureaucracy has found a simple solution—they use the public corporations' boards of directors as havens for retired bureaucrats. This system is what the Japanese call "amakudari"—descent from heaven. Many of the SLEs are called "sleeping legal entities" which have no other function than to pay salaries to retired bureaucrats. As one example, the Milk Transport Equipment Leasing Association is headed by a

[8]Johnson, p. 45.

[9]Gordon Tullock, "Dynamic Hypothesis on Bureaucracy," *Public Choice*, Spring 1974, pp. 127–31. For empirical evidence in support of this hypothesis for the U.S. economy, see James T. Bennett and Manuel Johnson, *The Political Economy of Federal Government Growth: 1959–1978* (College Station: Center for Education in Free Enterprise, 1980), pp. 27–55, and Thomas J. DiLorenzo, "An Empirical Assessment of the Factor-Supplier Pressure Group Hypothesis," *Public Choice*, Winter 1981, pp. 559–68.

[10]In other words, lobbying, like any other activity, is subject to the law of diminishing returns.

former general director of the Food Agency. Even though a board of audit found in 1969 that the association had engaged in absolutely no activity of any sort, the Ministry of Agriculture still included several hundred million yen (several hundred thousand dollars) in its budget for the association's support.[11]

The system of amakudari has come about because of the rapid growth of the Japanese bureaucracy and the nature of the government seniority system. Between 1932 and 1946, the number of bureaucrats grew from 109,888 to 256,218, and this kind of growth has continued. Japanese bureaucrats are promoted regularly by seniority and by class (most are graduates of Tokyo University, although a very small percentage is provided by other universities). However, promotion is only automatic up to a certain (section chief) level. After that, only a few members of each class can hope to advance. Furthermore, it is the government's policy that when members of a class are appointed to some of the highest posts (vice minister, director general, etc.), the members who do not make it must resign. The rapid expansion of the Japanese lower-level bureaucracy obviously created great pressures (from lower-level bureaucrats) for those in the top posts to retire early, after only a few years' service at that level, to make room for the burgeoning masses waiting to take over. Most vice ministers and other top officials do resign by age 55, but some stay on longer by eliminating talented people in classes immediately junior to theirs or by finding *them* jobs in public corporations.

In sum, the system of early retirement and the expansion of public corporations as "retirement havens" allows Japanese bureaucrats to avoid reductions in, or slower growth of, pay levels which would come from an ever-increasing size of the bureaucracy. The early retirees are simply "taken care of" through another budget, the FILP. Without the FILP, the self-generating growth of the bureaucracy would be much more limited.

Other important outlets for retired Japanese bureaucrats are the boards of directors of private corporations. For example, in 1974 the president of New Japan Steel was Harai Tomisaburo, MITI vice minister between 1953 and 1955; the executive director of the Tokyo Electric Power Company, the largest private electric power company in the world, was Ishihara Tokeo, MITI vice minister between 1955 and 1957; the executive director of Toyota Motor Company was also another MITI vice

[11]Johnson, p. 103.

minister, Yomamoto Shigenobu.[12] Thus, government control and regulation of Japanese industry has provided government bureaucrats with a lever to induce private corporations to create slots for retired bureaucrats on their boards of directors. The highly praised Japanese gift for cooperation and the avoidance of conflict between government and business is just as likely to be the result of bureaucratic manipulation through the "descent from heaven" process as it is of cultural forces.

Is There a "Japanese Disease"?

The Japanese government, in mid-1982, revised downward its economic growth forecasts after experiencing a 3.5 percent decline in real GNP during the first quarter—the first such decline in 30 years. And Japan's productivity, while still rising, is half the rate of growth of a few years ago. The drop in Japan's productivity growth has been even steeper than in the U.S. or Western Europe. Furthermore, Japan's savings are down a full third from the average rates of the 1970s. As a result of all these recent events, Professor Peter Drucker reported that on a recent trip to Japan his Japanese friends were saying, "In another four or five years, we will speak of the 'Japanese disease,' as 10 years ago we spoke of the 'English disease' and three years ago the 'American disease.' "[13]

The reason for Japan's economic stagnation, according to Drucker, is the same as that for other highly developed democracies—the crowding out of private borrowers from the capital markets and excessive regulation. Throughout its years of rapid economic growth, from the early 1950s to the mid-1970s, Japan's general account budget was either in balance or in surplus. Japan shifted to deficit spending in 1975, and the economy quickly slowed down. The general account deficit is now three times larger than it was seven years ago, and is larger in both per-capita terms and as a percent of GNP than the deficit of any other highly industrialized country except Canada.[14] But the shift toward deficits in the general account budget is only a part of the crowding-out problem, which depletes the necessary savings for capital investment and economic growth. Savings accounts and pension funds which are placed into the FILP and other government-controlled "second budgets" also redirect savings to finance current expenses and amount

[12]Ibid., p. 109.
[13]Drucker, p. 28.
[14]Ibid.

167

to more than half of the current account budget. The activities of the off-budget "public corporations" have contributed to the sharp decline in savings and capital accumulation, and Professor Drucker stated that the "archvillain" is the Japanese National Railway Corporation, which has a deficit equal to 18 percent of the Japanese budget!

The growing off-budget bureaucracy is becoming more powerful politically. Currently Japan is one of the youngest of all the developed countries with about seven percent of the population over 65. But by 1987 it is expected that Japan will have the same age structure as the West, with about 12 percent of the population over 65, which would entail an explosion in pension costs—promoting an even further drain on savings.

It appears, then, that Japan is beginning to experience the economic stagnation that has accompanied the growth in government in other highly industrialized economies, and this stagnation is being accelerated by the activities of the thousands of off-budget public corporations in Japan.

Off-Budget Enterprise in Israel

In Israel, numerous off-budget "public corporations" are owned wholly or partly by the national and local governments. Scores of other corporations are owned by the Histadrut, the labor union federation, which is legally distinct from the government but retains close ties with it and has exerted much influence over it. "Government corporations" in Israel are created by parliamentary ministers as a means of evading budgetary and civil service restrictions.[15] There are hundreds of such corporations owned by the national government, such as the Israel Aviation Corporation which employs over 16,000 workers, Israel Chemical Corporation, and Israel Coin and Metals Corporation. Similar OBEs exist at the municipal level of government including at least 12 in Jerusalem and 27 in Tel Aviv. Israel's public corporations can be created or eliminated by the government's purchase or sale of shares in various companies. When the conservative Likud Party came to power in 1977, after nearly 30 years of rule by the socialist labor parties, it was committed to reducing the size and scope of the public sector, which entailed liquidating government holdings in various corporations. However, the Likud Party soon found that such a task was nearly impossible, since most of the public corporations are a means of off-

---

[15]Ira Sharkansky, *Wither the State? Politics and Public Enterprise in Three Countries* (Chatham, N.J.: Chatham House Publishers, 1979).

budget financing of subsidies to the constituents of parliamentary ministers. After a year and a half, the Likud Party had not sold any more shares than had the previous Labor Party government, and had only one company on its "For Sale" list.

The Histadrut owns over 2,000 corporations which employ about 23 percent of the Israeli work force and account for 20 percent of net national product. These corporations are heavily subsidized and influenced by the national government and engage in a wide range of activities including manufacturing, banking, pension-fund management, hospitals, agricultural cooperatives, and many others. Since Histadrut corporations provide a means of off-budget financing of jobs and other benefits, political parties compete quite intensely in national elections for places on the national council of the Histadrut.

Another form of off-budget enterprise activity in Israel is the politically run foundation. The Jerusalem Foundation, for example, was established by the mayor of Jerusalem, who controls it, as a means of avoiding government spending constraints. Funds are solicited to finance projects which had previously been rejected by voters, such as swimming pools, sports stadiums to be used on the Sabbath, archaeological excavations, art studios, and numerous others. The Jerusalem Foundation is also subsidized by the national government.

The off-budget activities of government corporations have serious implications for the Israeli taxpayer. A huge portion of the nation's resources are allocated by various public managers who are isolated from any electoral constraints. The fact that the Histadrut alone owns over 2,000 corporations, which produce 20 percent of NNP, implies that the off-budget public sector in Israel is not likely to be diminished and will confound any attempts to reduce the burden of taxation in Israel, which is the highest of any democratic country in the world.

Summary

This brief survey of off-budget operations in various nations is certainly not exhaustive. Such entities exist in France and Italy as well as other developed nations. Even underdeveloped countries have adopted this form of "shadow government" to achieve political goals. The problem of assessing the extent of off-budget operations is due, in large part, to the desire of politicians to shield the spending, borrowing, and employment of the public sector from the prying of voter/taxpayers. Thus it is essential that there be further research on the operation of OBEs and their economic and political implications.

IX. Conclusions

Much of the appeal of fairy tales is that they always have a happy ending. Regardless of the trials, tribulations, and obstacles to be overcome, good triumphs unerringly over evil so that "they all lived happily ever after." There is always some turn of events, however improbable, that alters the balance of forces in favor of truth and justice. Up to a point, the story unfolded in this study is like a fairy tale—if one is willing to accept the notion that taxpayers represent good and politicians personify the forces of evil. Early in the 19th century, politicians in the state legislatures went on a spending spree financed by a bonanza of borrowing. Although the projects financed were supposedly undertaken in the public interest, many politicians became even more wealthy and, when the speculative bubble burst with the taxpayers holding the bag, there was in many cases little of substance to show for the expenditures. At this stage of the plot, iniquity appears to have triumphed. But to the rescue came the constitutional constraints on state government debt to protect the taxpayers, bringing justice for all. During the next decades, episodes like this were repeated with a different cast of characters. The taxpayers remained in the role of the good guys while local politicians played the heavies. Again, wanton borrowing led to municipal default and bankruptcies, which left taxpayers on the hook. Deliverance came from the state legislatures, which placed statutory and constitutional restrictions on the issuance of local debt.

So far, so good; but, alas, all did not live happily ever after. For the politician, the benefits from borrowing and spending were too great to be resisted. Because voters were leery of public debt, a method was needed that permitted the issuance of bonds without voter approval. At the turn of the century, in Maine, the technique was perfected to the satisfaction of the court: The public sector could establish corporate entities which not only could borrow, but could also ignore all restraints on debt imposed by statutory or constitutional means. The sole limitation was that tax revenues could not be directly pledged to pay the debt service and operating expenses of these quasi-public corporations; rather, their revenues had to be obtained from user fees and service charges—a limitation that has eroded steadily over time as massive amounts of subsidies and grants have been poured into the coffers of these off-budget enterprises. The courts' attitude toward OBEs has always been schizophrenic: OBEs were not *really* public agencies; if they were, debt limits would apply; but they were public agencies to the extent that tax-exempt bonds could be issued. Although it was regarded as inappropriate by the courts for the taxpayer to be *legally* bound to repay their debt, it has been quite proper for the taxpayer to be held *morally* responsible for OBE finances.

The off-budget device exists in a sort of twilight zone where it has reaped all the benefits of public-sector powers and privileges without being bound by the checks and balances that exist in the public sector, presumably to protect the interests of the taxpayer. Taxpayers have had no success in the courts in protesting the actions of OBEs and are unlikely to make headway in the future: The use of off-budget devices is so widespread and the financial stakes are so enormous that any serious legal threat to OBEs would send shock waves through the entire public sector and the financial markets. Witness the brouhaha that occurred when the citizens voted in Washington State to bring the Washington Public Power Supply System's future borrowing under voter control.

An increasingly tolerant and flexible attitude by the courts toward off-budget activities, and the active encouragement (in the form of loans and grants-in-aid) of the federal government during and after the Great Depression, provided an active stimulus to politicians to go off-budget on a major scale. The lure of federal dollars was too great a temptation (not that temptation was necessarily needed) and provided elected officials with a strong selling point to constituents: If certain activities were not undertaken, various forms of federal largesse would be lost. The genie was out of the bottle, imbued with mystical powers to incur debt, even in the presence of debt limits and without the consent of the voters. It permitted the activities of government to grow while the politician promised a smaller, less intrusive, and more fiscally responsible government. For the politician restrained in his activities on the one hand by the stringent constitutional limitations on debt and on the other by voters who viewed debt referenda with suspicion and despised tax increases, the legal acceptance of off-budget finance was pure sorcery.

OBEs constitute a shadow public sector that rivals, at least in borrowing, the on-budget public sector at the state and local levels. As the statistics presented in Chapter III clearly show, there is more off-budget long-term debt outstanding than voter-approved long-term debt. Moreover, in terms of new borrowings, OBEs are issuing nearly three times as much debt as general purpose governments. Like the broom that belonged to the sorcerer's apprentice, OBEs have a tendency to get carried away with their activities, spurred toward growth by a collection of special interest groups that benefit from such expansion. Every OBE has an active constituent group, including its managers and employees, willing and able to lobby actively for its programs, and none would gain from the demise of the off-budget entity or from a reduction in its activities. The case of the Washington Public Power Supply System amply illustrates the excesses that can occur when imprudence and incompetence go unchecked in an off-budget environment at the local level. The spendthrift experiences of New York State also reveal that it is all too easy for off-budget borrowing to get totally out of control. Regardless of the legal fiction that taxpayers are not ultimately obligated to shoulder the financial burden of OBE debt, practice has proven that, in one way or another, the piper must be paid and payment typically comes from the public purse.

Taxpayers in one political jurisdiction may occasionally take some comfort from the fact that the burden of a financially failing OBE may be passed on to other taxpayers, at least in part. When federal funds are used to shore up a municipal OBE, then all taxpayers in the nation carry the financial load while residents of the municipality obtain the benefits. Similarly, state funds may be used to save a local government off-budget enterprise so that all state taxpayers share the losses. A reasonable prediction is that, in due time, federal funds will help rescue WPPSS; years may go by before the system generates any electric power, and ever-increasing utility rates will lead to anguished pleas for federal assistance on a massive scale. The deep involvement of the Bonneville Power Authority provides both a rationale for such aid and a vehicle through which it may be passed. Continued bailouts of OBEs may weaken further the incentives that currently exist for these entities to be self-financing. If political gains from borrowing and spending are not eroded by having the burden of a failing OBE fall directly on those who receive the benefits, threatening bankruptcy to get federal hand-outs may become part of the OBEs generally accepted *modus operandi*. Even though such a prospect is hardly appealing, the precedent has already been set by the case of New York City.

Our focus on the problems of such OBEs as WPPSS and New York's Municipal Assistance Corporation is not motivated by a desire to tell horror stories, although the sagas of these and other OBEs would provide ample material for just this purpose, or perhaps for a Keystone

Cops script. These organizations are atypical only in the sense that vast amounts of debt and extremely poor management are involved. Many other OBEs are also in financial straits even though, for political reasons, outright bankruptcies and default on debt are very rare. The notion that OBEs are run in a businesslike manner is a myth. Not only are the routine competitive pressures that exist in the private sector largely, if not totally absent, but also political considerations permeate the functioning of every OBE. Experience has repeatedly shown that those politically expedient actions are often not in the best interest of taxpayer and voter.

Few politicians would be candid enough to proclaim that political objectives compete with the public interest in off-budget activity. Indeed, even we do not assert that taxpayers do not benefit from OBEs. Clearly, many of the activities in which they engage are important and necessary to the functioning of both society and the economy. The central issue is why these activities should be placed off-the-books. To suggest that OBEs are more efficient, less encumbered, and more flexible than the standard government agency is hardly an acceptable answer. If on-budget government is so inefficient, encumbered, and inflexible, why not advocate a thorough revamping of bureaucracy? A major overhaul of the public sector certainly would do no real harm and might do a great deal of good. The suggestion that off-budget organizations are so superior to general-purpose government can be interpreted as an admission by politicians that they are poor managers of their administrative agencies—hardly a novel idea, but it casts some shadows that elected officials would prefer to avoid.

We are as likely to see a marked improvement in the functioning of the public sector as we are a balanced federal budget—it's perennially promised, but rarely produced. The taxpayer should be concerned, however, about the inherent inefficiency that exists in every bureaucracy and should demand improvements. Even if OBEs were far more flexible and efficient organizations than government agencies, voters should view them with skepticism and distrust for a very simple reason: The voters have no direct control over the directors or the managers of OBEs, no veto power over their actions, and no control over their borrowing and spending. Even elected public officials—the "agents" of the voters—have only minimal control over off-budget entities, for once the board of directors is appointed and the OBE formally established, it can lead its own existence, although tax or rate payers may be either legally or morally obligated, explicitly or implicitly, to make the organization financially viable. Thus, a nonelected group of political

174

appointees is entrusted with determining which actions are, in fact, in the public interest. This function no longer belongs to the voters or taxpayers. The electorate has lost control of a large segment of public-sector activities, and as the case studies developed in earlier chapters clearly show, the consequences can be disastrous. As the tax revolt simmers or gathers steam, the political benefits increase from placing as much public-sector activity as possible off-the-books.

The political incentive for budgetary magic is nowhere more evident than at the federal level. The almost innocuous Budget Act of 1974 did nothing whatever to limit spending or federal revenue. All the law required was that target levels of total spending be specified in the budget process. Yet the response was immediate in terms of off-budget activity. From (by federal standards) a very modest beginning, off-budget activities skyrocketed at an astounding rate. Growing concern over federal budget deficits led to placing the Strategic Petroleum Reserve off-the-books and, in a desperate attempt to make the deficit projections more palatable, the Reagan administration even floated a trial balloon to see if placing the Social Security System off-budget would "play in Peoria." It didn't, but this action would have lowered the reported deficit.

The primary reason that off-budget finance is relatively new at the federal level is that effective constitutional constraints on borrowing have never been imposed upon Congress. Access to the credit markets has always been virtually limitless. The tax revolt of the 1970s, however, gave Congress pause—especially since more than 30 states had called for a convention to add a balanced budget amendment to the Constitution. The pressure grew for Congress to disguise as much of the deficit as possible and to distribute federal largesse through such vehicles as loan guarantees rather than as outright grants or subsidies. OBEs at the federal level are subject to the same maladies as those at the state and local levels of government: Witness the sleight-of-hand performed by TVA to cover its excessive inventories of nuclear fuel.

There is one recurring theme throughout this study: History has shown that statutory and constitutional limits on debt can be, and on a large scale have been, evaded by politicians at the state and local levels. Those frustrated taxpayers who expect a balanced budget amendment to the Constitution to work miracles in controlling federal spending are, if the past is any guide, likely to be very disappointed. Most federal politicians have served in public office at the state and local level where the OBE device has been raised to an art. It is purely wishful thinking to believe that the off-budget potential for federal programs has been overlooked or exploited to the fullest extent possible.

This gloomy assessment of the likely effectiveness of constitutional constraints on federal borrowing is reinforced and emphasized by the fact that Congress has refused to obey its own laws mandating a balanced budget. Section 7 of Public Law 95-435 (Bretton Woods Agreements Act) approved October 10, 1978, specifically states that "Beginning with fiscal year 1981, the total budget outlays of the Federal Government shall not exceed its receipts." In simple and direct terms, this statute requires a balanced budget, but no positive progress has been made toward this goal; if anything, federal deficits have soared and prospects for future progress are increasingly dim. Failure to abide by the law cannot be dismissed as congressional oversight, because a second law (Public Law 96-5) mandating a balanced budget was approved in 1979. Federal politicians who refuse to obey their own statutes can hardly be expected to accept the restrictions of a constitutional amendment. Most of the proposed amendments have ample loopholes (e.g., the balanced budget requirement can be overruled by a three-fifths majority vote) and lack any enforcement powers.

It is not our intent to debate the pros and cons of different stipulations of proposed constitutional amendments requiring a balanced budget, but rather to point out that no change to the constitution is likely to be very effective in constraining taxes, revenues, and borrowing by the federal government if it is not enforced, and if politicians themselves are not held liable for constitutional subversions. A constitutional amendment would make it more costly and more cumbersome for members of Congress to achieve their political goals, but it would by no means halt the practice of employing the public purse to reward special interest groups at the expense of the taxpayer. In effect, the record dramatically demonstrates that there are severe limitations to legal constraints on the fiscal affairs of government.

The public sector has by no means passively accepted the taxpayers' desire for lower taxes and less government. Instead, the public sector has responded to the tax revolt by moving its activities off-budget and concealing the employment, spending, and borrowing that an expanding government entails. Elected officials have found off-budget devices to be ideal vehicles for furthering their political objectives. The taxpayer has lost effective control of a very large and rapidly growing portion of the public sector's activities, yet implicitly is obligated to bear the burden of its financial excesses.

The underground government produces many economic distortions in that certain activities and organizations are subsidized at the expense of others, rent seeking and rent avoidance are encouraged, over-investment is rewarded in those endeavors which produce revenue in excess of costs for OBEs, and political factors rather than market forces determine the allocation of resources. There is no way to measure the costs imposed on society by off-budget devices; indeed, even the full extent of off-budget activity is unknown, but looking at that tip of the iceberg that can be detected, it is apparent that the total costs are very substantial.

At this juncture, convention dictates that an incisive solution to the problems identified be set forth. The Gordian knot must always be cut. In all candor, we confess that we have no simple solutions for eliminating the political propensity toward profligacy in a democracy once and for all. The major point of this exercise has been to show that surefire solutions even in the form of constitutional constraints have not been entirely successful over a period of more than three-quarters of a century. Fiscal constraints have not been enforced, and there is no such thing as a "self-enforcing" constitution. There is no yellow brick road which leads directly to political utopia.

Although a balanced budget amendment to the U.S. Constitution is unlikely to provide an answer for all time to the problem of political profligacy, it could have very beneficial effects in the short run. Politicians who are able to remain in office are astute and, as Senator Everett Dirksen once observed, when they "begin to feel the heat" they "begin to see the light." Public pressure that results in adoption of a balanced budget amendment would at least impress on members of Congress the intensity and depth of sentiment toward government spending and borrowing. In effect, such an amendment could have a very important psychological impact on politicians by diminishing their enthusiasm for plunder of the public purse. After all, history shows that once constitutional constraints were adopted at the state and local levels, several decades passed before the off-budget mechanism was discovered and made operational. Even then, more decades passed before OBEs were adopted on a wide scale. It is entirely reasonable to suggest that government spending at the state and local levels was restricted to some extent as a result of the legal obstacles that were imposed. The crux of the problem is that politicians and bureaucrats have enormous incentives to find alternative routes around the statutory and constitutional roadblocks placed in their path. These incentives will always exist in a democracy and, as a result, it is impossible to draft a constitutional amendment that is "foolproof" or "failsafe" in the sense that

177

it will effectively constrain the fiscal actions of the federal public sector for all time: There is truth in the cliche that "where there is a will, there is a way."

It follows from the reasoning above that any constitutional amendment mandating a balanced budget will be effective only in a limited sense, for three reasons. First, politicians and bureaucrats will, over time, find ways to bypass even the most rigid limits on their fiscal actions. Interpretation and implementation of the amendment will lead to the development and exploitation of loopholes. Second, there is no way at present to enforce the amendment, i.e., neither members of Congress nor bureaucrats are rewarded for fiscal responsibility or punished in some sense for fiscal irresponsibility. It is hardly reasonable to propose that members of Congress be shot at dawn if the federal budget operates in the red, but some incentives are essential if the goal of balanced budgets is to be achieved. A suggestion that has intuitive appeal is to make the salaries of public employees and politicians dependent in some way on whether the budget is in balance. If the income of those responsible for federal budgets falls dramatically whenever the budget is not balanced, the likelihood of balanced budgets will increase markedly. Third, it is essential that a better understanding be obtained of what is meant by a "balanced budget"; one of the most critical aspects of this research has been to show that when federal revenues equal federal expenditures, the budget is *not* necessarily "in balance." Much of the off-budget activity does not require outlays by the government, e.g., loan guarantees. Despite the fact that there is no explicit accounting entry, subsidies are involved in such cases, even though the exact dollar amount of the subsidies is not explicitly known. Similarly, regulations impose real costs on the economy and may implicitly be regarded as taxes, even though the magnitude of the costs is unknown and the "revenue" is never reported as government income. In short, when off-budget items are taken into account, the whole question of what *is* the federal government budget becomes extremely complex. There is no way that a simply worded and easily understood statement requiring a balanced budget can take into account these complexities and control for them. Recall also that the off-budget activities of state and local governments rival in size and scope the on-budget activities of general-purpose governments. It would be a grave mistake to assume that off-budget devices may be safely ignored when a balanced budget constraint is specified.

Thus, although a constitutional amendment may be an important first step in bringing government spending under control, it would be shortsighted to assume that such a step would provide a long-term solution to the nation's fiscal problems. As time passes, the amendment would have to be reexamined and refined so that political attempts to subvert its intent could be offset. The principal role of the economist in fiscal reform is to anticipate the actions of public-sector entrepreneurs in circumventing the constraints imposed on their actions and then to devise even more effective rules. These rules must be accompanied by an incentive structure or an enforcement mechanism which ensures that the rules adopted will be followed.

It is essential that economists develop a better understanding of the mechanics of off-budget devices and their effects on economic activity. Methods do not now exist for the taxpayer (or, indeed, even the politician) to track or analyze the total impact of federal fiscal activity, and until such methods are devised—a very difficult, if not impossible task—the monitoring and control of federal spending, taxing, and borrowing cannot be executed with any degree of confidence. Indeed, it is difficult even to make rational budget decisions under such circumstances.

Finally, a major goal must be the education of the taxpayer, who should be concerned about the motivation for and consequences of actions of the public sector at all levels of government. This book is intended as a contribution to this education process and, although it does not contain the answers to all the relevant issues, it does raise substantive questions that should provide grist for the researchers' mill for years.

EPILOGUE

Underground Government: The Off-Budget Public Sector is a book that everyone interested in the operations of the public sector and the behavior of elected officials needs to read. It is particularly timely because it provides many insights that are relevant to the role of government in contemporary America. Many of our citizens now are aware that the public sector has expanded far too rapidly in size and scope and interferes unnecessarily and wrongly in all our lives. The issue is no longer whether the role of government should be reduced, but rather what methods are likely to be most effective in limiting a government that is getting out of control.

As the authors correctly observe, the tax revolt is a clear sign of voter unhappiness with elected officials and the policies they have fostered. Disillusionment with the public sector is widespread, for taxpayers see clearly that government has increasingly become wasteful, inefficient, and unresponsive to citizen demands. Bennett and DiLorenzo persuasively argue that taxpayers have become so frustrated by officeholders that they are no longer satisfied with trying to reduce the tax burden at the ballot box, but instead are taking a course of action which has much more serious and far-reaching implications: They are refusing to pay taxes by "going underground"—by not filing tax returns and by under-reporting income when they do file. As such practices become more widespread, others are encouraged to evade the payment of taxes. So pervasive is this underground economy that the federal government alone is estimated to lose more than $100 billion in revenue in 1982. Moreover, since unreported income and employment are not counted in the official statistics, unemployment is overstated, and income and productivity understated. These erroneous statistics lead to erroneous policy prescriptions that exacerbate rather than ease the nation's economic ills. It is imperative that public spending be brought under control so that the burden of taxes becomes tolerable. But to do this, budget reform is urgently needed and, in my opinion, long overdue.

The authors discuss the adoption of a balanced budget amendment to the Constitution as a policy tool for stemming the growth rate of the federal government and bringing spending under control. But we must

181

go on to ask, "Will a constitutional restriction work in practice?" It is in this area that this book is particularly useful. Bennett and DiLorenzo have researched the experience of statutory and constitutional constraints at the state and local levels of government, and their work demonstrates that, over a period of almost a century, such limitations have had very little impact on the expansion of the nonfederal public sector. They show that politicians, because they benefit from increased spending, have managed to move large segments of the public sector "off the books" where neither spending nor debt limitations apply. Such budgetary magic is accomplished by creating public corporations called authorities, boards, commissions, and trusts, which now exist in great numbers throughout the U.S. The authors refer to such corporations as "Off-Budget Enterprises" (OBEs). The use of these devious methods is wrong. If it were done in private enterprise, those responsible would find themselves in court.

Underground government has truly ominous implications for the American taxpayer. These off-budget enterprises issue vast amounts of debt—more state and local borrowing is now done off-budget than on-budget—and the spending of OBEs rivals that of official state and local budgets. We often forget that whereas on-budget borrowing requires the approval of voters in a referendum, off-budget borrowing needs no voter approval whatever. Furthermore, the directors and managers of OBEs are political appointees, rather than elected officials. Thus, as the public sector has increasingly moved off-budget, the electorate has lost the ability to control directly much of the economic activity or the policy decisions made by the unelected managers of OBEs.

It is often said that OBE borrowing does not require voter approval because repayment of principal and interest is accomplished from revenues generated by the OBE's operations, e.g., toll revenues from bridges or highways. But Bennett and DiLorenzo convincingly demolish the myth that OBEs are financially self-supporting. In fact, they show that taxpayers support these off-the-books operations through massive grants and subsidies. In-depth case studies are explored at both the state and local levels of government to illustrate the excesses that so often have occurred (and still are occurring) when the public sector is able to operate beyond the scrutiny of the voters. Because the employment and spending of OBEs do not appear in the budgets of the governmental jurisdictions that created them, the size of the public sector at the state and local levels is grossly understated. It should also be brought to the attention of readers that many of the activities of off-budget enterprises compete directly with private sector firms and,

182

because OBEs are permitted to issue tax-exempt bonds, they borrow at favorable rates, which crowd private borrowers out of the markets for capital. The authors do far more than document the existence of the off-budget public sector; they estimate its size and scope and also examine the economic and political consequences.

In contrast to the state and local public sector, the federal government has moved toward off-budget activities only in the past decade. Prior to the 1974 Budget Act, which attempted to introduce rationality into the federal budgetary process, there was virtually no off-budget spending. Since then, it has grown rapidly (by more than 30,000 percent in less than a decade) by moving some federal enterprises off the books, by an increasing reliance on loan guarantees, and through the activities of the Federal Financing Bank. Federal politicians are motivated by the same self-interest that pervades state and local elected officials: the desire to reward constituent and special-interest groups while dispersing the costs of programs among all taxpayers and deferring the costs by borrowing.

As pressures mount for spending reductions and limitations on borrowing, the authors predict that federal politicians will engage in the same type of behavior that state and local politicians have practiced for decades—there are ample incentives to encourage the disguising of federal financial activities. The rather limited evidence available to date clearly indicates that Bennett and DiLorenzo's prediction is valid. Although a constitutional amendment may dictate that all expenditures and debt activity undertaken by the federal government be subject to its restrictions, there are still no ironclad guarantees that members of Congress will not be able to circumvent even carefully specified constraints on their behavior. Every rule must be implemented and interpreted; no rule is self-enforcing. The interpretation and implementation of rules permit the development and exploitation of loopholes and, if enforcement is lax (or nonexistent), it is impossible to "close" the loopholes. None of this should be interpreted to imply that a constitutional amendment restraining spending or borrowing is of no value, but merely to indicate that there are no "quick fixes" or panaceas to a major problem facing not only the citizens of the U.S., but also the citizens of every nation in the world. In the short run, at least, constitutional limitations make it more difficult for politicians to continue to use the same methods to further their self-interest that have been used in the past. Moreover, if public sentiment demands such limitations, elected officials will think twice before running roughshod over them.

As Senator Everett Dirksen once perceptively observed, "When a politician begins to feel the heat, he begins to see the light."

Underground Government provides an in-depth treatment of many issues that are fundamental to a comprehensive understanding of the contemporary public sector, how it has developed, and how it is likely to evolve in the future. Although, as Bennett and DiLorenzo candidly admit, they do not have all the answers to the numerous questions raised throughout this book, they have developed a thought-provoking study that should be of major interest to all who are concerned about the size, scope, and role of government in the U.S. today.

WILLIAM E. SIMON

ABOUT THE AUTHORS

James T. Bennett is Professor of Political Economy and Public Policy at George Mason University in Fairfax, Virginia. He received his Ph.D. from Case Western Reserve University in 1970 and has specialized in research topics related to public policy issues, the economics of government and bureaucracy, and labor unions. He has published more than 50 articles in professional journals such as the *American Economic Review, Review of Economics and Statistics, Public Choice, Cato Journal*, and *Policy Review;* other books include *The Political Economy of Federal Government Growth* (1980), *Better Government at Half the Price* (1981), and *Deregulating Labor Relations* (1981). He is an adjunct scholar of the Heritage Foundation and a member of the Philadelphia Society and the Mont Pèlerin Society.

Thomas J. DiLorenzo is Assistant Professor of Economics at George Mason. He received his Ph.D. from Virginia Polytechnic Institute and State University in 1979. His research interests include public choice, state and local public finance, labor economics, and public policy. He has published numerous articles in such professional journals as *Public Choice, American Economic Review, Public Finance Quarterly, Southern Economic Journal, Quarterly Review of Economics and Business, Journal of Labor Research, Policy Review, Cato Journal*, and *Review of Social Economy*. He is an adjunct scholar of the Cato Institute.

The Cato Institute

The Cato Institute is named for the libertarian pamphlets *Cato's Letters*. Written by John Trenchard and Thomas Gordon, *Cato's Letters* were widely read in the American colonies in the eighteenth century and played a major role in laying the philosophical foundation for the revolution that followed.

The erosion of civil and economic liberties in the modern world has occured in concert with a widening array of social problems. These disturbing developments have resulted from a failure to examine social problems in terms of the fundamental principles of human dignity, economic welfare, freedom, and justice.

The Cato Institute aims to broaden public policy debate by sponsoring programs designed to assist both the scholar and the concerned layperson in analyzing questions of political economy.

The programs of the Cato Institute include the sponsorship and publication of basic research in social philosophy and public policy; publication of the *Cato Journal*, an interdisciplinary journal of public policy analysis, and *Policy Report*, a monthly economic newsletter; "Byline," a daily public affairs radio program; and an extensive program of symposia, seminars, and conferences.

CATO INSTITUTE
224 Second St., S.E.
Washington, D.C. 20003